NORTHERN IRELAND: STUDIES IN SOCIAL AND ECONOMIC LIFE

Northern Ireland: Studies in Social and Economic Life

edited by
RICHARD JENKINS

Avebury in association with the
Economic and Social Research Council

Published by
Avebury

Gower Publishing Company Limited
Gower House
Croft Road
Aldershot
Hants GU11 3HR
England

Gower Publishing Company
Old Post Road
Brookfield
Vermont 05036
USA

British Library Cataloguing in Publication Data
Northern Ireland : Studies in social and
economic life.
1. Northern Ireland. Social conditions
I. Jenkins, Richard, *1952–* II. Economic
and Social Research Council
941.60824
Library of Congress Cataloging-in-Publication Data
Northern Ireland : studies in social and economic life / edited by
Richard Jenkins.
p. cm.
Chiefly papers presented at a conference, held at Queen's
University of Belfast, Jan. 6–7, 1987.
Includes bibliographies and index.
1. Northern Ireland–Social conditions–1969–Congresses.
2. Northern Ireland–Economic conditions–Congresses. 3. Northern
Ireland–Rural conditions–Congresses. I. Jenkins, Richard, 1952–

HN398,N6N674 1989   88-26007
941.6082'4–dc19   CIP

ISBN 0 566 07027 8

Contents

PART IV *URBAN COMMUNITIES AND SOCIAL POLICY*

Preface
Richard Jenkins

Between 1980 and 1983, the Northern Ireland Research Initiatives Panel of the Social Science Research Council (now the Economic and Social Research Council) funded a range of research projects in the province. Under the chairmanship of Professor Michael Wise, with a membership drawn from the academic community on both sides of the Irish Sea, and from trade unions and the business world in Northern Ireland, the Panel was largely concerned to support research into social and economic problems in Northern Ireland.[1]

The Panel's brief was explicit in its attempt to encourage research into issues other than sectarian conflict or problems of law, order and security. These were areas in which SSRC felt that research had already been strongly enough supported by organizations such as the Ford Foundation, perhaps to the detriment of other, equally important topics. This was thought to be particularly the case with respect to economic policy-related areas of interest. The Council's view concerning these issues was formed, at least in part, by representations from civil servants at Stormont who perceived a lack of support for this kind of research in Northern Ireland, by comparison with other United Kingdom regions. In those representations, and the discussions which they generated, can be seen the origins of the Panel and its funding policy.

Right from the beginning of the Panel's activities this policy – the avoidance of research about, or related to, 'the Troubles' – was very controversial. With the benefit of hindsight, it is easy to make a personal judgement and say that the policy was misguided. However, at the time it appeared to offer a fruitful and novel way into the 'problem' of Northern Ireland. In particular, it seemed to me, certainly, to hold out the prospect of allowing one to approach these questions: what is distinctive about Northern Ireland and to what degree, and in what respects, is it the same as, or broadly similar to, its neighbours, Great Britain and the Republic of Ireland? In addition, there were undoubtedly areas of research activity in Northern Ireland – economics is an obvious example – which were underdeveloped and which stood to gain much from the Panel's work.

There are, I think, three main reasons for a degree of retrospective dissatisfaction with the Panel's funding policy. First, it is clear that sectarian conflict and the ethnic divide are such all-pervasive aspects of life in Northern Ireland that there are few social or economic research topics which do not, of necessity, require their recognition and consideration. Adopting such a perspective need not, however, have conflicted with the Panel's approach, which, let us remember, only excluded research whose *central* theme was, in whatever sense, 'the Troubles'. In fact, the Panel did fund research which explicitly took account of the communal divide: Leo Howe's work on unemployment, the project led by Tom Lovett, looking at youth service provision and participation, and Alan Middleton's research into small businesses, are good examples.

Second – and this is less easy to document – it was then, and remains now, my strong impression that many of the most experienced and most able local researchers were either discouraged from applying to the Panel for research funds, or had their applications turned down, precisely because their research interests lay firmly in the areas which the Panel had decided not to support. Since the major social issue in Northern Ireland is 'the Troubles', this, while unfortunate, should not surprise us.

Finally, there is, once again with the benefit of hindsight, an argument to be made that an intitiative such as the Panel, which in large part responded to research grant applications from established academics – rather than, say, funding postgraduate studentships or endowing centres of developing research excellence – is not the best way to stimulate activity in areas where it is felt to be lacking. If research in a particular area – whether it be a substantive topic or a discipline – is underdeveloped, then that is in itself likely to indicate an absence or shortage of the kind of established and experienced researchers from whom fundable grant applications will be forthcoming. Certainly, where the Panel did depart from its reactive or responsive mode, as in its modest programme of youth work research or its more substantial financial contribution to the setting up of the Northern Ireland Economic Research Centre (see Chapter 6), its efforts appear to have been more successful in encouraging the growth of a local research base.

In 1986 the evaluation and dissemination phase of the Panel's programme was begun, under the supervision of the present author. In addition to the commissioning of reports on various aspects of the Panel's work by specialist assessors, a major part of the dissemination exercise was a conference on 'Economic and Social Research in Northern Ireland' which was held at the Queen's University of Belfast on 6 and 7 January 1987. More than 150 participants, drawn from a variety of disciplines and from both parts of Ireland and Great Britain, attended the meeting. The papers in this collection are a selection from the presentations.

Four plenary sessions offered the conference broad overview perspectives on various aspects of research in Northern Ireland. These papers, written specifically for the occasion, are printed here in full. Liam O'Dowd, in Chapter 1, offers a more detailed exposition than I have provided of the perils of ignoring the communal divide and the implications of so doing for social research in Northern Ireland. John Darby, in his discussion of social policy research in the province in Chapter 2, makes some of the same points. Graham Gudgin in Chapter 6, proposes a research agenda for economic research in Northern Ireland and R.H. Buchanan looks at research into rural society in Chapter 3. This latter area is, of course, of enormous importance: despite the looming presence of Belfast, both in the local consciousness and in the eyes of the world outside. Northern Ireland remains a largely rural society, albeit one with a significant network of small towns (not to mention Derry).

The conference proved to be the forum for the exchange of a wide variety of sometimes sharply opposing views and analyses. Eighteen papers deriving from Panel-funded research were presented, covering everything from the marketing of Northern Ireland's seed potatoes to youth culture, small manufacturing firms to the landlord–tenant relationship in the private housing sector.

Bearing in mind the diversity of these topics, it is not easy to summarize adequately the nature and content of the debate within the formal sessions and elsewhere. There were, however, a number of recurrent, and largely shared, themes which emerged.[2] With apologies to those who so forcefully argued some of these points, lest I be thought to distort as well as summarize, these were as follows.

The theme which emerged most noticeably and which commanded most collective assent has already been referred to: trenchant criticism of the policy which had excluded conflict-related research from the Panel's terms of reference. Many of the best local researchers, being strongly committed to research into aspects of sectarian conflict, were, as a consequence, effectively excluded from the panel's programme. A further line of argument – perhaps most elegantly expressed in Liam O'Dowd and John Darby's plenary sessions – stressed the difficulties of ignoring the conflict when doing most kinds of social research in Northern Ireland.

A second question which was raised, in one form or another, over and over again is related to the first issue. As John Darby asks in Chapter 2, what is distinctive about Northern Ireland? In what respects is the province different from, or the same as, Great Britain and the Republic of Ireland (or, indeed, other parts of the world)? Liam O'Dowd posed the issues in concrete terms by arguing for a research perspective which encompasses studies of the conflict without allowing it to dominate or mesmerize the enterprise.

Other people, Graham Gudgin among them, highlighted the concentration in existing research upon the area east of the River Bann, particularly upon the greater Belfast urban area. Many people, either from the platform or the floor, pointed to this imbalance. As has already been mentioned, Ronnie Buchanan's paper highlights the scope for further research in small towns and rural areas. Belfast, as one participant pointed out, is *not* Northern Ireland. Although sterling work has been done in rural communities by geographers and social anthropologists, here is an obvious avenue for future research development.

Finally, the role of the Economic and Social Research Council in fostering collaborative research efforts with organizations and researchers in the Republic of Ireland was clearly an issue of considerable importance. Robert Cormack and Robert Osborne, in their paper,[3] and Professor John Jackson, in his remarks from the floor, forcefully made the point that more could be done in this respect. This is all the more relevant in the light of recent moves by the Royal Irish Academy to encourage social and economic research throughout the island.

The papers included in this volume are, with the exception of the contributions from Buchanan, Darby, Gudgin and O'Dowd, the result of research supported by the SSRC Northern Ireland Panel. It is only a selection, however, of both the Panel's programme and of the papers presented at the conference. It is to be hoped that they will provide encouragement for further discussion and research, both inside and outside Northern Ireland.

Notes

1. Although the author was a member of SSRC Northern Ireland Research Initiatives Panel, the views expressed in these introductory remarks do not in any sense represent the other members of the Panel or the Economic and Social Research Council.
2. Perhaps the best context within which to explore these themes is the wider literature on Northern Ireland. Good places to start are F.W. Boal and J.N.H. Douglas (eds), *Integration and Division* (London: Academic Press, 1982); J. Darby (ed.), *Northern Ireland: The Background to the Conflict* (Belfast: Appletree Press, 1983); P. Teague (ed.), *Beyond the Rhetoric* (London: Lawrence and Wishart, 1987) and B. Rowthorn and

N. Wayne, *Northern Ireland: the Political Economy of Conflict* (Cambridge: Polity, 1988). For comparative purposes, a useful survey of society in the Republic of Ireland is K.Λ. Kennedy (ed.), *Ireland in Transition* (Cork: Mercier, 1986), while a good collection of papers concerned with all of the island's 32 counties is *Ireland: A Sociological Profile*, ed. P. Clancy, S. Drudy, K. Lynch and L. O'Dowd (Dublin: Institute of Public Administration, 1986).

3. Bob Cormack and Bob Osborne's paper is not included here. The SSRC Northern Ireland Panel funded a conference on 'Social Policy: North and South', held in Belfast in December, 1984 and organized by Cormack and Osborne. The conference proceedings were published as a special issue of *Administration* (vol. 33, no. 3, 1985).

Contributors

Tim Blackman, Department of Social Administration and Policy, University of Ulster at Coleraine.

R.H. Buchanan, Director, Institute of Irish Studies, The Queen's University of Belfast.

Paul J. Bull, Department of Geography, Birkbeck College, University of London.

Reginald Byron, Department of Social Anthropology, The Queen's University of Belfast.

John Darby, Director, Centre for the Study of Conflict, University of Ulster at Coleraine.

Roy Dilley, Department of Geography, University of St Andrews.

Wendy Garner, Ulster People's College, Belfast.

Norman Gillespie, Policy Research Institute, Belfast.

Graham Gudgin, Director, Northern Ireland Economic Research Centre, Belfast.

R.I.D. Harris, Department of Economics, The Queen's University of Belfast.

Leo Howe, Department of Social Anthropology, University of Cambridge.

Richard Jenkins, Department of Sociology and Anthropology, University College of Swansea.

Joe Larkin, The Sports Council, London.

Tom Lovett, Director, Ulster People's College, Belfast.

Alan Middleton, Faculty of the Built Environment, Birmingham Polytechnic.

Liam O'Dowd, Department of Social Studies, The Queen's University of Belfast.

John E. Spencer, Department of Economics, The Queen's University of Belfast.

Julie M. Whittaker, Agricultural Economies Unit, University of Exeter.

PART I
KEY ISSUES IN SOCIAL RESEARCH

1 Ignoring the communal divide: the implications for social research
Liam O'Dowd

In Northern Ireland the Protestant–Catholic division shapes the way people vote, where they live, go to church and school. It influences their experience of both work and leisure. The communal divide also shapes what is meant by such terms as democracy, majority rule, discrimination, peace, violence, terrorism, even politics. In ordinary everyday language, terminology is used by both sides of the divide to possess, exclude and express collective solidarity. Language is infused by communal division in a manner often taken for granted by the insider and opaque to the outsider. Yet Northern Ireland is not to be understood simply as a unique or anomalous entity, it has always been part of a wider world. It is precisely the interaction between communal division and the wider world which social research must elucidate if it is to make a worthwhile contribution to social understanding and policy-making.

The wider world is not to be understood as something simply 'external' to the province in geographical and structural terms. Rather, it constitutes Northern Ireland in an important sense. Thus, the Protestant–Catholic divide has developed in conjunction with British colonial settlement and empire, with the industrial revolution, urbanization, the welfare state and the changed role of the British state in the world-system. Class, occupational and locality structure has been married from the outset to changing communal relations. The march of modernization, capitalism and welfarism, far from obliterating communal division, has reshaped and reconstituted it. Similarly, communal divisions have shaped the concrete forms of environment, economy and society in Northern Ireland. It is this interweaving of communal division, environment, economy and politics which has given Northern Ireland its particular stamp.

The distinctiveness of Northern Ireland within the UK is underlined by the endemic difficulty of compartmentalizing questions such as law and order, the constitution, the boundaries of the state, from day-to-day life, i.e. from 'normal' politics, economic and cultural life.

In general, social research has been reluctant to grasp this central fact. Within the spectrum of social research on the province, two poles have evolved, each of which, in different ways seeks to deny it by strategies of avoiding and/or compartmentalizing communal division and the Troubles. This has greatly limited the contribution of social research both to understanding Northern Ireland and to policy formulation.

At one pole, the outbreak of the Troubles has prompted social scientists to see Northern Ireland's distinctiveness as residing purely in the depth, ubiquity and intensity of Protestant–Catholic division – a division that since 1920 has assumed the status of a national division. What has made Northern Ireland different and interesting to social science is what has made it newsworthy, i.e. the obvious manifestations of conflict such as marches, violence and the army on the streets. Initially, therefore, the Troubles attracted experts on political conflict, violence, terrorism and insurgency (see Rolston et al., 1983). The following discussion does not deal with this research in detail, rather it registers its tendencies to concentrate on the 'abnormal', to render the Troubles synonymous with communal relations, and to compartmentalize 'Troubles-related' issues from 'normal', economic and class issues.

I wish to concentrate here on research at the other pole. The underlying strategy of this research has been epitomized by the initiative of the SSRC's Northern Ireland Panel. Here, probably the most substantial social research initiative ever undertaken in the province attempted to address 'normal' problems such as employment, unemployment and housing while deliberately avoiding 'abnormal' or contentious issues such as aspects of the sectarian divide, security and what has become euphemistically known as 'the Troubles'. The strategy was clearly to concentrate on issues which are in Richard Rose's (1971) terminology 'bargainable' – which might be of common concern – while avoiding the 'non-bargainable' issues which divide.

In what follows I wish to submit that such a strategy, however well intentioned it might be, seriously undermines whatever contribution social research might make to analysing Northern Ireland. At best, it is an understandable attempt to direct attention to areas neglected by the rush to study the Troubles. At worst, it indicates a desire to avoid controversial research based on a wilful ignorance of the problematical links between economics, politics, social organization and culture in the province.

First, let me enter some qualifications to this argument. The following is not, in fact, a discussion of the SSRC's Northern Ireland Panel initiative, rather my aim is to examine the wider implications of the type of overall research strategy which informed it. This strategy of avoiding or comparmentalizing the Troubles and communal division did not originate with the SSRC/ESRC nor is it currently peculiar to it. Indeed, it pre-dates the Troubles. It is certainly not my intention here to assess any of the research carried out within the parameters of the initiative, even if I were competent to do so. I am fully aware that some of the projects at least (examples include Howe's and Lovett's research reported elsewhere in this volume) did directly confront the problems of communal division even if the parameters of the overall strategy scarcely encouraged them to do so.

The discussion is organized under four broad headings:

(1) An examination of the historical and structural factors which have underpinned a research strategy which seeks to concentrate on the 'normal' and avoid and/or compartmentalize communal division and the Troubles.
(2) A refutation of some of the more explicit arguments which have been advanced in favour of strategies of avoidance and compartmentalization.
(3) A brief discussion of two research areas – studies of the regional economy and fair employment research to illustrate the arguments in the first two sections.
(4) An outline, of the implications, in rather summary form, of what I would see as an alternative and more fruitful research strategy.

Historical and structural conditions of research

Strategies of avoidance or compartmentalization have been encouraged by at least three historical and structural factors: (i) the nature of the academic community in Northern Ireland, (ii) the type of state administrative policy prevailing, and (iii) the structure of everyday interaction in the province. Prior to the Troubles, outside social science interest in Northern Ireland was minimal. Internally, empirical social research in the social sciences was poorly developed with the partial exceptions of geography and economics. With a few honourable exceptions (see, for example, Jones, 1960; Barritt and Carter, 1962; Harris, 1972) the nature, depth and intensity of communal division in the province was simply ignored. It was not seen as an academically respectable pursuit. Indeed, there was resistance to any intellectual interest in Northern Ireland in some quarters. Not only was there resistance to studying communal divisions, there was also a resistance to studying the common ground. Perhaps it is Estyn Evans, the geographer, archaeologist and anthropologist, who has done more than any single academic in Northern Ireland's history to inspire research into a common Ulster heritage of the physical environment and popular culture. In a long career here between 1928 and 1970, the resistance he met (on his

own account) from university and ecclesiastical circles seems to
have had two sources, neither of which is as yet completely extinct
(interview with author and Evans, 1984: 10).

One was on a pseudo-cosmopolitan disdain for the local and the
mundane. This disdain was linked to a metropolitan bias among
some who saw themselves in temporary exile in a remote backwater
of the UK. A certain ambivalence towards according local and Irish
subjects due weight in a British-oriented university curriculum only
began to be remedied after the 1950s with the development of the
social sciences, the rapid growth of Catholic students in university
and the growing international interest in the Troubles (Scott, 1973;
Taylor, 1986). The other source of resistance to empirical research
derived from local political and sectarian myth-making about the
past which was only too eager to project current divisions back to
the dawn of time. Evans' work did inspire many students and local
historians. He was able to link his local research to broader international concerns (e.g. Evans, 1957; 1973). Almost by definition,
however, his work avoided the immediacy and intensity of the
political and cultural divisions enshrined in the Northern Ireland
state. It was a research perspective which inevitably left out or
greatly diminished the immediacy of questions surrounding power
and ethnic-sectarian divisions.

It was precisely these questions, when violently exposed in the
1960s and 1970s, which generated the massive interest of
international social science in Northern Ireland. This led one
observer to suggest that social scientists seem to have been
mesmerized by the Troubles (Jenkins, 1984). By 1983, it was
possible to compile a social science bibliography of well over 5000
publications on Northern Ireland which had been published since
1945 – the vast majority since the 1960s (Rolston et al., 1983).

As the Troubles persisted, the social science disciplines became
more established locally, and as the study of Northern Ireland
became more respectable academically, local and often better
informed contributions began to be made to the international social
science literature.

The localization of research effort did bring in to sharp focus,
however, the problems of researching a conflict situation while
actually living here permanently. Whereas prior to the mid-1960s
communal division and indeed Northern Ireland generally was
largely avoided by social science, by the late 1970s a rough division
of labour was emerging between those studying 'normal problems' –
allegedly matters of common interest to both communities – and
those studying the Troubles. The former seemed easier to do and
seemed to offer a more positive local counterbalance to the fixation
of visiting researchers. It is possible to interpret the Northern

Ireland Panel initiative as an attempt to strengthen this focus in ways that might be useful to policy-makers. As the Committee for Social Science Research in Ireland was then devoting some resources to studying the 'Northern Ireland Problem', it seemed opportune no doubt to focus on the 'problems of Northern Ireland'. The academic division of labour, now more developed within the province, ensured that some disciplines saw the Troubles/communal division as falling outside their remit, to be consigned perhaps to the dustbin of the rather more unscientific disciplines such as sociology, history, anthropology and political science. Indeed, the Northern Ireland Panel was to allocate relatively little money to these disciplines.

Secondly, after 1974, local research began to echo some of the concerns of a Direct Rule administration which was far more bureaucratic and centralized than its Stormont predecessor. Apparently disenchanted with the prospect of agreement between local political parties, the Northern Ireland Office emphasized the merits of running the province fairly and efficiently as just another regional unit of the UK. Reading official pronouncements of the time, it seemed that what distinguished Northern Ireland from other UK regions was a higher than average unemployment rate and higher rates of certain types of crime.

The old Stormont, like the Dublin administration prior to 1960, had felt little need for empirical social research. Under Labour Direct Rule, this changed. If Northern Ireland was to be treated as any other part of the UK, there was scope for empirical investigation of topics such as parity of administrative provision with the rest of the UK. More research began to be carried out locally which often avoided, or at least sidestepped, communal conflict. The SSRC research initiative was a product of this period. Interestingly, by the early 1980s, this compartmentalization was to be modified again as policy-makers began to stress the ubiquitous effects of communal division and political instability even with respect to local economic decline (O'Dowd, 1985). A stronger commitment to monitoring Catholic and Protestant comparisons is now reflected in the work of government researchers (see, for example, the Continuous Household Survey; Department of Economic Development, 1986).

There is a third and very significant structural incentive to avoid and compartmentalize the Troubles and communal division in NI. This arises from the structure of everyday communal interaction to which social scientists and administrators conform, as well as the 'man on the street'. This is what Burton (1978) has termed 'structured non-communication', i.e. the tacit assumption that avoiding contentious issues such as 'politics' and religion, or at least an agreement to treat them in a perfunctory and stereotyped manner, is a *sine qua non* for viable cross-communal interaction. Much sociological and anthropological research has shown that this pervades both working-class and middle-class settings, even if it often more subtle in the latter. The whole process is predicated on an ability to use an accumulation of social cues to 'tell the difference'. The result is different sets of rules for inter- and intra-communal interaction.

This discussion of the historical and structural conditions which are conducive to the avoidance or compartmentalization strategy has been intended to show that these strategies are not simply arbitrary, nor do they arise in every case from the ignorance of social researchers.

I wish to turn now to consider more explicit arguments advanced in support of the avoidance or compartmentalization strategies:

(1) the principled objection – religion does not really matter and in any case should not matter in the late twentieth century;
(2) the politics of communal division makes related research dangerous and threatens social scientific impartiality;
(3) communal division is intractable – why not concentrate on what unites people rather than what inexorably divides them?
(4) conflict research has in any case produced little of relevance for either social science or policy-making.

Religion does not really matter and in any case should not matter
This view may be found in approaches which see the conflict in narrowly political, economistic or class terms. To many from outside Northern Ireland religion is a small part of the secular world having to do with personal beliefs and worship. In Northern Ireland, it is a badge, very important in its own right for many people, but more generally a badge recognized by all as standing for particular traditions and historical realities. These have fused experiences of settlement and colonization, and of class, political power, violence and attitudes to the state. The notion that the type of communal or religious identification found in Northern Ireland is somehow unique can be quickly dispelled by a cursory look at the not too distant history of Britain and Ireland as a whole, or by a glance at similar conflicts in a wider comparative perspective.

Communal conflict makes related research dangerous and threatens the impartiality of all social science
There is no doubt that the nature of the conflict does place limits on some research – on paramilitaries, the police, and prisons, for example. The most detailed studies of republican paramilitaries,

prison life and security forces' undercover work have not been
produced by academics but by journalists, participants and others
with special access, There are obvious physical and legal dangers, as
well as problems of access, with respect to in-depth research into
the role of the security forces and paramilitaries. Even so, some
social science research has proved possible on these and other
contentious topics (e.g. Nelson, 1984 on loyalist paramilitaries).
Furthermore, researchers such as Burton (1978), Wiener (1980) and
Jenkins (1983) have studied local communities heavily pervaded by
the conflict. The threat of such research to social scientific
impartiality, is surely outweighed by the strain on credibility were
'dangerous' subjects to be ignored altogether.

*The communal division/Troubles are fundamentally intractable,
therefore why not concentrate on what unites rather than divides?*
While avoidance may be based on lack of access or fear, it may also
be rooted in the profound conviction that, at root, the communal
divide is non-bargainable and intractable. As Rose (1976) suggests,
the problem is that there is no solution. There is a danger that this
approach merely feeds intractability by leaving it unchallenged. A
belief that compromise, in a broad and undifferentiated sense, is
impossible may encourage social researchers in their avoidance of
contentious issues. If logically developed as policy prescription it
can mean admitting that one side or other must be coerced – a
sometimes unpalatable idea to some liberal-minded social scientists.
I am not underestimating here the appeal of intractable positions, a
force suspected by many of the 'avoiders'. Neither would I
underestimate the major role of coercion or force in communal
relations, in the creation and maintenance of Northern Ireland, or
in the opposition to it as a separate unit. Instead, I would argue
that social research here can and must study the many forms of
coercion which do exist and their different implications, not only for
shaping intractable political positions but for wider socio-economic
realities in the province.
    The second part of the intractability argument suggests
concentration on those limited issues which unite rather than
divide. This is a view which appeals to many, both as a strategy
and an adequate empirical assessment of the situation. There is
some justification for this view. There are matters of immediate
common concern to both communities, e.g. nuclear pollution,
unemployment, social welfare, etc. Yet even here, not far beyond a
general consensus, familiar differences on priority and strategy soon
re-emerge. Of course, the fact that the history of Northern Ireland
is littered with examples of the limits, even of the failures, of
attempts to establish common ground, is no reason to abandon

them. It might be argued that without such attempts the divisions would be much deeper. Yet it remains the job of the social scientist to probe precisely why consensus is so limited, - why for example, so much well-intentioned and selfless effort often appears utopian and naive. To turn a blind eye to conflict and coercion is to ensure that the efforts to build consensus and common interest are doomed to marginality in the long run.

There is also a sense in which avoiding the intractable issues may mean that they are smuggled into 'normal' research by the back door. One of the key premises of popular and intractable sectarianism, i.e. that Protestant–Catholic divisions are zero-sum in nature - if one side gains, the other side loses. Of course, this ignores the possibility that gains for one side may eventually lead to gains for all (the fixed cake may get bigger) - a possibility also neglected in much social research.

There are, of course, some plausible grounds for such zero-sum thinking. They arise from the importance of the sectarian 'head count' in electoral politics, communal attempts to control territory seen as a fixed resource, and the belief that there is a fixed number of jobs to go round. Importantly, here, some social science perspectives, which operate with rather mechanical views of scarcity, confirm such views whether they explicitly deal with communal division or not. Examples include the extent to which all social sciences share the basic assumption of scarcity enshrined in neo-classical economics and geographers' emphasis on 'territory' as a scarce resource for which both communities compete.

All this is not to deny the force of zero-sum thinking, rather it is to recognize that social researchers have a choice of either uncritically confirming it and leaving it unchallenged on the one hand, or employing parameters and approaches which do challenge it on the other. I shall come back to this point in an illustration later.

It is deluding to take refuge in apparently 'scientific' and universalistic notions like 'scarcity' and 'competition' without recognizing the politics of their application in Northern Ireland. The questions asked, the geographical parameters of the study, even some of the terminology used can be quickly decoded in Northern Ireland anyway, however 'scientific' and neutral they may appear to the uninitiated. The links between politics (broadly defined) and social research generally have been fully recognized in most countries. To ignore them in Northern Ireland is particularly perverse given:

(a) the all-pervasive role of the state as a direct employer, provider of assistance to the so-called private sector, and as a source of education, health, social services, housing and security.

(b) the centrality of the struggle over the boundaries of that state, its legitimacy and who controls its institutions. (I make a distinction here, of course, between state and government.)

Conflict research has contributed little either to social science or to policy formulation

In 1983, Professor John Whyte, in an inaugural lecture at Queen's, asked the question: 'Is Research on the Northern Ireland Problem Worth While?' While noting the massive volume of such research, his conclusions were on the whole very pessimistic. He argued that politicians and civil servants rarely read research on the 'Northern Ireland Problem' and when they did they got precious little enlightenment from the (at least twelve) extant and often conflicting interpretations of the conflict. While he acknowledged the potential utility of some highly specific problem-oriented research, his case for research rested mainly on the potential of NI as a stage for testing general social science theories and, to a lesser extent, the hope of aiding future scholars. Thus the main justifications advanced were academic and scholarly rather than policy-related.

Whyte had good grounds for pessimism about the immediate utility of research in Northern Ireland. It might be argued however that he started, by implication at least, with an excessively ambitious hypothesis, namely that social research could directly contribute to the 'solution' of the Northern Ireland Problem. In all countries, the relationship between social research and policy-making is seldom immediate, direct or uncomplicated. The problem is compounded in Northern Ireland by the existence of overt political conflict, the differential opportunities for evaluating various government policies and above all by the tendency to compartmentalize research on 'normal' issues from issues related to communal divisions.

To a considerable extent, this tendency is shared by those who focus on violence and the political conflict directly. Instead of systematic attempts to analyse the connections between economics, politics and culture, the debate often resolves itself into a battle over which labels to apply to the essence of the Northern Ireland Problem – for example, is it about economics, class, religion, colonialism, nationalism, ethnicity, racism, or terrorism? The answers are often too directly embedded in the questions asked and reflect the politics (often implicit), discipline and degree of exposure to Northern Ireland, of the observers concerned. Diminishing returns can soon become evident in many of these debates.

The critique of avoidance and compartmentalization strategies may be illustrated by reference to two research areas. The first arises from the economic analysis of Northern Ireland, the other from research connected with fair employment strategy.

The regional economy

The development of official economic analyses of the regional economy is particularly instructive when viewed in the light of the strategies of avoidance and compartmentalization discussed above. Quantitative techniques have been developed further in economics perhaps than in any other discipline and, in many of its manifestations at least, it is wary of focusing on local political and cultural variables. In spite of this, Northern Ireland economic analysis has had to live with a progressive politicization of the economy – in the sense that the province has become a state-dependent and state-centred economy (O'Dowd, 1986).

Economic analyses of the 1950s and 1960s scarcely registered the economic implications the communal divide or that the peculiar nature of the state might have implications for its regional planning strategy (see, for example, Isles and Cuthbert, 1957; Wilson, 1965). Questions such as labour mobility, the location of industry and infrastructural developments, even expanding public expenditure, were loaded with implications for the politics of communal relationships and for public policy. Yet, these were ignored.

In the 1970s and 1980s, there were two developments. First, economic analyses began to be peppered with allusions to the negative effects of violence and political conflict. Phrases such as 'the security situation', political instability, 'return to normality' and the 'bad image of NI' became commonplace (O'Dowd, 1985). Economists seemed reluctant to explore in detail what these phrases might mean or to register relevant research by other social scientists.

Gradually the Troubles began to be introduced into analysis as a relatively undifferentiated variable to help explain the fall-off in jobs arising from foreign investment and their partial replacement by jobs engendered by the conflict. Secondly, the growing focus on unemployment made it increasingly difficult to avoid the communal division as it became clear that there were durable structural differences in Catholic and Protestant rates. The Quigley Report (1976) marked a substantial advance in that it recognized the centrality of state decisions for the economy. Its stress on the dual economy east and west of the Bann suggested an indirect recognition of the economic relevance of communal division.

It remains the case, however, that there is a reluctance to engage in systematic empirical investigations of the relationship between economic and socio-political factors. Avoidance has been replaced by a muted recognition and compartmentalization or by the sometimes problematic use of geographical variables as proxies for communal affiliation.

It seems clear historically that the industrialization of Northern Ireland has helped form the communal divide and has in turn been shaped by it. The same points can be made about subsequent de-industrialization and the rise of the state-centred regional economy. Government policy has pinned most of its hopes for economic revival on small indigenous and localized enterprise, the intertwining of business and communal relations are surely relevant to the prospects of success. Without this type of analysis, there is the danger that economists, painstakingly empirical and precise in narrowly 'economic' analysis, may operate on the most inadequate and untested assumptions about social and political questions. The reverse is true for non-economists.

Fair employment research
My second illustration is a related one. It has to do with research stimulated by questions of inequality in employment and legislative initiatives to deal with it. Negative reactions to this type of research recall some of the points made above about ignoring the politics of communal division:

(a) The charge that it exacerbates divisions. Clearly investigations of job bias and the changing Protestant–Catholic composition of those employed and unemployed can encourage crude checklists of gains and losses – the type of zero-sum philosophy I criticized earlier. It is important that researchers do not give uncritical credence to this view but they can hardly be blamed for its existence. As part of a powerful popular sectarianism, it would exist without fair employment research anyway albeit without the benefit of accurate information.

(b) The view advanced by some administrators, employers and even social researchers that 'religion' is and should be of no interest. One of its commoner manifestations is to contrast meritocracy to the whole messy and irrelevant business about 'religion'. Yet much local and international research on job recruitment reminds us that meritocracy is far from the unproblematical term its most vociferous advocates claim. Clearly in some cases degrees of merit are clear. But in many jobs they are not: here all kinds of tacit understandings about personality, reliability and attitude, of huge potential significance in a divided society like Northern Ireland come into play. Furthermore, in some cases, informal recruitment and judicious job specification can be used to ensure that some kinds of 'merit' are rewarded more than others. Recent research here by Cormack and Osborne (1987) has shown that similar educational credentials do not necessarily mean similar levels of job opportunity for Catholics and Protestants. The principle of merit is valuable but its mere assertion can obscure the practical ambiguity which surrounds it.

Fair employment research is an awkward reminder of how central the politics of sectarian headcount is in Northern Ireland. Multivariate analysis of communal differences can sometimes be used in rather unconvincing fashion to avoid the full implications of this. It can statistically attempt to explain away communal differences in unemployment rates, for example. It can be shown that some of the difference may be explained by factors such as social class, location and differential fertility even if religious affiliation is still an independent influence. This type of analysis is important but it can obscure the communal experience of all these variables simultaneously. The Catholic or Protestant unemployed are not likely to see unemployment in such analytical and rational terms as the would-be research analyst. Statistical relationships should not be confused with concrete communal relationships on the ground. Injunctions from policy-makers or social scientists to migrate, emigrate or adopt more temperate reproductive behaviour are not only patronizing and paternalistic, they can be proxies for the crudest forms of popular sectarianism, Northern Ireland-style.

The great potential contribution of fair employment research is that it can help put on the agenda some of the obscure links between class, employment, politics and culture. These links need to be investigated much more systematically. Fair employment research under the aegis of the Fair Employment Agency, has helped clarify the distinction between intentional discrimination and structural disadvantage. It is no longer possible to argue that communal division is simply the product of prejudicial ideas carried around in people's heads. Certainly each side has prejudicial (if different) ideas about the other but division is deeply rooted in differing material circumstances – in class, work and unemployment profiles and in the durable and asymmetrical power relations associated with them.

Research on the communal divide also demonstrates the degree of internal differentiation in both communities and at least provides a basis for assessing how the chemistry of internal division helps to produce the overall divide. The recognition that the communal divide is both shaped and, in turn, affects state institutions can lead to systematic empirical research of relevance to public policy. To be worthwhile, this research cannot automatically assume that the state is a neutral arbitrer dedicated to consensus-creation between two warring factions. The state is neither completely 'external' nor is it monolithic. With political pressure and the vast expansion of the state's role, its institutions have increasingly incorporated both sides of the communal divide. The new emphasis on monitoring communal representation in the public and private sectors (Department of Economic Development, 1986) is a welcome first step to assessing the extent and ramifications of change. A realistic appraisal of public policy must examine both the contentious and divisive aspects of state policy as well as those which encourage consensus. It must also recognize that the effects of policy may diverge from the intentions of the policy framers.

Conclusion: Towards an alternative strategy
The argument, then, is not that every specialized research project has explicitly to study communal relations or the Troubles. It is rather that such projects should be informed by an overall framework which links the so-called normal and abnormal features of society in Northern Ireland. I am not suggesting either that all research must conform to a grand social theory. Instead, I am arguing that Northern Ireland provides a challenge to work more at the interface of existing social science disciplines while seeking to break some of the moulds which shape prevalent understandings of politics in the province. Furthermore, research needs to be continually aware of the way in which the language of social science intersects with everyday language of communal division.

I have suggested that the 'distinctiveness' of Northern Ireland should not be seen to reside simply in the Troubles, nor in the nature of communal division, but in the way they interact with 'normal' social issues. Recast in this way, the study of Northern Ireland is more realistic, not just in local policy terms, it can also tell us much about aspects of the past, present, and perhaps the possible futures of the rest of the UK and the Irish Republic.

Integrating communal relations into social analysis does not necessarily mean that class and gender relations, for example, are thereby less important. Indeed there is some evidence that class and communal divisions may be mutually supportive in practice. Furthermore, it is wrong to imply that communal division is synonymous with the Troubles, to see it as simply pathological or as 'abnormal'. It is folly to wish it away given its durability.

The problem for social research is surely to examine communal division in a multifaceted way. This means assessing the full effects of different manifestations of communal division. Some of these are negative, others simply point to the integrity of a communal identity based on a particular set of historical relationships and experiences. It is true that part of the identity on one community is to be different and opposed to the other. But it is here that social research can help to disentangle the relationships of subordination and domination from those of interdependence. Superficial assumptions and claims about common interests are counterproductive. Common interests there are but these can only be fully recognized when the obstacles to realizing, expressing and working towards them are fully researched. No one social science discipline is sufficient for this task.

Social research cannot solve the Northern Ireland problem, but neither can it solve or even adequately address 'normal' problems in isolation from the Northern Ireland problem. It can expose the fallacies in the cosmopolitan and Olympian view of Northern Ireland, i.e. that the province is caught in a time-warp in which two equally intransigent tribes confront each other – one a mirror-image of the other. It can also challenge some of the most powerful and simplistic ideas inherent in popular sectarianism locally. For social scientists, full recognition of the centrality of communal division may help to distinguish popular sectarianism from the durable ethnic sectarian divide. Without this recognition, social research may be either irrelevant or used crudely as ammunition in the inter-communal struggle.

Even a tentative specification of popular sectarianism reveals its potential for suffusing social research if often at the level of tacit assumption. The key elements of sectarianism might include the following:

(1) the view that the struggle is simply a zero-sum struggle;
(2) the perception that the struggle is between two undifferentiated and unchanging entities locked in an intractable and enduring struggle;
(3) that history is an unending cycle of rebellion and coercion, coercion and rebellion; and
(4) a narrow and impoverished concept of politics as having to do with flags and emblems, marches and arches.

It is only by challenging the strategies of avoidance and compartmentalisation so common in existing social research that some innovative thinking can be encouraged about conditions under which the sectarianism can be separated from the integrity of Protestant–Catholic division. It may even uncover some of its more positive features.

Acknowledgement

I would like to thank John Whyte for helpful comments on an earlier draft of this chapter.

Ignoring the communal divide: 17

References

Barritt, D.P. and Carter, C.F. (1962) *The Northern Ireland Problem: A Study in Community Relations*, London: Oxford University Press.

Burton, F. (1978) *The Politics of Legitimacy: Struggles in a Belfast Community*, London: Routledge & Kegan Paul.

Cormack, R.J. and Osborne, R.D. (1987) *Religion, Occupations and Employment, 1971-81*, Research Paper 11, Belfast: Fair Employment Agency.

Department of Economic Development (1986) *Equality of Opportunity in Employment in Northern Ireland, Future Strategy Options: A Consultative Paper*, Belfast: HMSO.

Evans, E.E. (1957) *Irish Folkways*, London: Routledge & Kegan Paul.

Evans, E.E. (1973) *The Personality of Ireland*, Cambridge: Cambridge University Press.

Evans, E.E. (1984) *Ulster: The Common Ground*, Mullingar: The Lilliput Press.

Harris, R. (1972) *Prejudice and Tolerance in Ulster: A Study of Neighbours and Strangers in a Border Community*, Manchester University Press.

Isles, K.S. and Cuthbert, N. (1957) *Economic Survey of Northern Ireland*, Belfast: HMSO.

Jenkins, R. (1983) *Lads, Citizens and Ordinary Kids*, London: Routledge & Kegan Paul.

Jenkins, R. (1984) 'Understanding Northern Ireland', *Sociology*, Vol. 18, No. 2, pp.253-64.

Jones, E. (1960) *The Social Geography of Belfast*, Oxford: Oxford University Press.

Nelson, S. (1984) *Ulster's Uncertain Defenders*, Belfast: Appletree Press.

O'Dowd, L. (1985) 'The Crisis of Regional Strategy: Ideology and the State in Northern Ireland', in G. Rees et al. (eds), *Political Action and Social Identity*, London: Macmillan.

O'Dowd, L. (1986) 'Beyond Industrial Society', in P. Clancy et al. (eds), *Ireland: A Sociological Profile*, Dublin: Institute of Public Administration.

Quigley Report (1976) *Economic and Industrial Strategy for Northern Ireland: Report of a Review Team*, Belfast: HMSO.

Rolston, B. et al. (1983) *A Social Science Bibliography of Northern Ireland: 1945-1983*, Belfast: Queen's University.

Rose, R. (1971) *Governing Without Consensus: An Irish Perspective*, London: Faber.

Rose, R. (1976) *Northern Ireland: A Time of Choice*, London: Macmillan.

Scott, R.D. (1973) 'University under Stress - The Peculiar Problems of Teaching in Ulster', *Vestes*, Vol. 16, pp. 127-33.

Taylor, R.L. (1986) *The Queen's University of Belfast and its Relationship to the 'Troubles': The Limits of Liberalism*, Unpublished PhD thesis, University of Kent at Canterbury.

Whyte, J.H. (1983) *Is Research on the Northern Ireland Problem Worth While?*, Inaugural Lecture, Belfast: Queen's University.

Wiener, R. (1980) *The Rape and Plunder of the Shankill*, Belfast: Farset Press.

Wilson Report (1965) *Economic Development in Northern Ireland*, Belfast: HMSO.

2 The prospects for social policy research in Northern Ireland
John Darby

The first beneficiaries of the ESRC Northern Ireland initiative were myself and two colleagues. We were asked, as a ground-clearing exercise, to produce a register of the economic and social research projects on Northern Ireland which had been started or completed between 1980 and 1983. The report found 516 projects (Darby, Dodge and Hepburn, 1983). It is impossible to tell how many were missed. Since then it is possible to point to a number of initiatives which have affected or are likely to affect the ways in which individual academics can carry out their research:

(a) First there was the greatly increased and threatening presence of the University Grants Committee - a bird previously rarely sighted in Northern Ireland - and the nervous rush towards evaluation and research specialization which is still going on.

(b) There was the merger between the New University of Ulster and the Ulster Polytechnic, which certainly increased the research potential of the university sector. But it also removed at one blow the polytechnic sector, raising the question whether its particular qualities have been carried on and nurtured.

(c) There has also been a growing dependency of researchers on government funding - already identified in our report - and the effect of subsequent and current cutbacks.

(d) There was the formation of the Northern Ireland Economic Research Centre and the Policy Research Institute, to facilitate and encourage cooperation between the two universities, cooperation not particularly common in the past.

(e) Finally there was the ESRC initiative, which has now been completed and which we are assessing in this conference. Has it altered the pattern of research activity? Should it have?

The point is that the ESRC initiative was carried out amid the most frenetic, alarming and radical changes in university research in recent times. How, in the middle of this turmoil and in the sure conviction that there is more to come, is one to approach a paper on 'the prospects for social policy research in Northern Ireland'?

The question cannot be approached holistically, so I intend to base my remarks on a basic premise and proceed from there. The premise is that there ought to be some level of equilibrium across the spectrum of conflicting interests involved in policy research. I am aware that anyone researching in this area might come up with a different set of equilibria, or different emphases, or challenge the notion of equilibrium itself. Having enunciated the principle, I can only indicate those areas of social policy research which seem to me to be in disequilibrium at the moment. There are five:

(1) the imbalance between different geographical settings, and especially between Belfast and the rest of the province;
(2) the imbalance between different academic disciplines;
(3) the imbalance between general concerns and local peculiarities;
(4) the imbalance between government funding and funding from other sources; and
(5) the imbalance between 'servicing' research and critical research; this is partly a consequence of the imbalance between public and private funding.

Geographical disparity
The first imbalance is the geographical disparity in research activity. The case for more emphasis on rural research is made by Ronnie Buchanan in Chapter 3. I want to endorse this, and add that the problem is not so much urban versus rural as Belfast versus the rest of the province. There is a powerful magnet, located in Belfast, which so pulls both researchers and funding bodies that, in research terms, Belfast is often used as a synonym for Northern Ireland. Of the 516 projects identified in our survey, only five were specifically concerned with the west of the province, and this includes the city of Derry. Enniskillen does not appear in the index. Yet the west contains the most stark and difficult of our economic and social problems. I believe that the reasons for this disparity are similar to those which have concentrated English research resources on the south at the expense of the north – an attitude of mind rather than a calculated choice. I can still remember the condescending amusement which greeted an early suggestion that the Policy Research Institute might be located outside the city.

There are now greater, and growing, research resources in the west due partly to the fact that the Magee campus of the University of Ulster is virtually the only area of substantial expansion in higher education. I hope that, in five years' time, this shift will be reflected in the flow of research funding and the balance of research activity.

The Belfast magnet is sometimes defended by pointing to the fact that about 40 per cent of Northern Ireland's population lies within the Belfast metropolitan area. The same mathematical formula indicates that 60 per cent do not.

Disciplinary imbalance

My second concern is the imbalance between favoured and neglected disciplines in the social policy field. This is illustrated by the 1983 Register where, for example, there was funding support for 90 per cent of projects in Agriculture and 68 per cent in social medicine. Less than half the projects in social studies and politics received any grant, and in some subject areas the proportion was much smaller. While this problem continues, it has been somewhat overtaken by other trends. There is a strong tendency in all institutions towards team and interdisciplinary research. On the whole I must admit to some sympathy for this development. The Centre for the Study of Conflict where I work is strongly committed to building up a strong nucleus of researchers working on related projects. Our experience has been that this sort of setting encourages an ambience genuinely conducive to research, where individual researchers are mutually supportive of each other and new ideas are sparked off – that the whole is better than the parts. But this approach is not appropriate to every project or every researcher. The danger in the headlong rush towards sometimes artificial and forced partnerships is that individual researchers, working on individualistic or non-conformist projects, may be trampled in the rush. What used to be a problem of imbalance between disciplines has become a danger of imbalance between individual and team research.

General versus peculiar

My third imbalance is not confined to Northern Ireland. The research being conducted in any geographical region ought to reflect both concerns which are common everywhere and those which are peculiar to the area. Thus in Northern Ireland one would expect to find social policy research being carried out into unemployment, housing, social conditions, industrial relations, etc. The peculiarities of Northern Ireland, however, are unusually dramatic. There is an abnormally high level of unemployment and abnormally serious social consequences; our peripheral position within the United Kingdom and Europe also raises peculiar difficulties; and there are the Troubles. If the research scales slide too sharply towards general issues, we neglect some of our most serious practical and theoretical problems. If they slide in the opposite direction we may become obsessed with the uniqueness of these problems and ignore the lessons to be learned from others. In the final analysis insularity may be the greater of the two dangers. My impression is that this balance is currently about right. But it was not helped by the artificial division made by the SSRC into violence-related and non-violence-related problems. The only justification for declassifying them is to emphasize the point that they are inextricably intertwined.

One prescription against insularity is comparative study and Irish social policy could hardly be better situated for it. Within the same island are two systems which sprang from the same roots, and have since diverged significantly. This ready-made case study may be relatively well covered in the teaching of social policy, despite problems of finding appropriate textbooks and data. But the question remains, why is there so little comparative policy research, not only between Northern Ireland and the Irish Republic, but of any sort?

The low level of interest in comparative study among funding institutions can only be part of the explanation, as EEC funding sources, which are tailor-made for such cooperation, are notoriously under-used in Ireland. The different research traditions on either side of the border are a more serious barrier. The International Fund may be disposed towards such research cooperation, and there are one or two instances of individual endeavours. As it stands, however, it is more common to find universities in Ireland linked with European and North American institutions than with each other. I can see few signs on the horizon that this situation will change in the next decade.

Government versus trusts: servicing or criticizing?

The fourth and fifth concerns are, in my view, the most serious, and are so closely related that I propose to discuss them together. They are first, the imbalance between research funded by government and that funded elsewhere; and second, the implicit consequent imbalance between research which services public policy and that which criticizes it.

When our review began there was already a clear disparity between areas receiving government funding and those less fortunate. It was our view that one consequence of direct government funding was a strong tendency towards 'servicing' research – that is, the analysis of data which would help the implementation of decisions already reached rather than more open-ended and potentially critical research into fundamental problems. This might be described as post-decision research rather than ante-decision research. Almost 90 per cent of university research into agriculture, for example, was supported by government funds. The resulting projects were predominantly short-term applied projects, were tightly coordinated and without overlap, but were also less likely than others to be critical of policy, or to consider long-term implications or the broader social and economic context in which the research was carried out. There were projects to examine the effects of EEC regulations on sectors of the agricultural industry, but no projects examining the EEC itself or the processes by which its policy decisions were reached.

There is nothing wrong with government funding per se. The Centre for the Study of Conflict has been awarded funding by both public and independent bodies. The public funding bodies with which we have been working have been remarkably open and supportive. They are sensitive to the need for independence in research, are knowledgable and willing to take on controversial subjects. Most important in this context, when the research parameters have been agreed, they have remained scrupulously non-interventionist.

So this is not a criticism of government funding, or of applied research. Indeed, one could argue that in some areas, like social medicine and agriculture, such an emphasis is not only likely but desirable. My concern is about the increasing dominance of government and quasi-government bodies in the funding of policy research *relative to other funding sources*. It has increased greatly in the last decade and is likely to increase in the future. I believe that the increased dependency of researchers on public funding is worrying for two main reasons.

(a)   The first is the increased financial vulnerability of research to the financial cuts which are current. Since the 1970s, for example, the Northern Ireland Housing Executive has become virtually the dominant generator of housing research. Some of this was commissioned out to independent researchers. In recent years, however, there has been a significant shift towards in-house research by the Executive and a consequent decline in independent housing research; one additional effect is that less of the research has been published and hence is not readily available to independent researchers, thus further diminishing the attractiveness of housing to potential researchers. Another recent example is the decision by the Department of Education, towards the end of last year, to reduce dramatically the funding available to the Northern Ireland Council for Educational Research, the main educational research body in Northern Ireland. What has been the effect of this haemorrhage of funding from educational research in the province? Has it been left anaemic and weak? The truth is that we do not know. The research constituency was not properly consulted before the decision; nor have alternative plans, if any, been announced.

In both these examples one funding body had become dominant during the years of relative plenty. But when they changed their approaches during the years of shortage their very dominance had ensured that there were few readily available alternative sources .

(b) An even more important effect of the greater government involvement in research is the potential danger of control. In many instances of research – perhaps most – there is no serious conflict of interest between the researchers and their funding bodies. Relationships remain close and consensual. But what if the research findings become critical of the funding body itself?

Let me give an example close to home. When my colleagues completed the register of research for the then SSRC in 1983 we insisted on prefacing it with an analytical essay. Among other considerations we examined the patterns of funding and had some criticisms, not only of government funding, but of the SSRC initiative itself. In particular we were concerned about the arbitrary division between conflict research and non-conflict research, the nonsense of which has surely now finally been nailed. These criticisms produced a letter from the then Director of the SSRC, however, asking rhetorically whether we seriously expected the SSRC to publish criticism of its own funding policies. Well, that is precisely what we should expect. But this instinctive protective reaction by one major funding body is perhaps the main reason why we should be alarmed at the growing dependency of policy research on a public funds.

So, during periods of financial and political caution, there may be a tendency to fall back on experienced researchers and conservative subjects. Both of these may militate against young researchers. How are they to get started in an atmosphere which demands specialisation and quick results?

I believe that there is a need for overall review, so that neglected areas may be stimulated, and neglected researchers in unfashionable areas can be supported. There are enough disadvantages operating against researchers at the moment. Let us exploit two of our main advantages – the peculiarities of our experience here, and the size of the province and its research population. Both should allow us to find an appropriate way of tackling our own problems.

How might this be approached? What are the alternative bodies who might provide such a mechanism? Obviously government is the least appropriate body to protect the idea of independent research. In the present financial situation can the universities be relied upon to do this? Perhaps the formation of the Policy Research Institute improves the chances, but the universities' own fights for solvency make it more difficult than before. That leaves the Trusts as the most likely bet.

In the last twelve years there have been two attempts to introduce a broad funding initiative on Northern Ireland: one by the Ford Foundation in the mid-1970s, the other by the SSRC. Rowntree and other Trusts have a proven concern with the province. I suggest that neither the researchers nor the Trusts can any longer afford to have these isolated initiatives remain isolated. There is urgent need for an amalgamated approach. The time has come for the major relevant trusts to come together and liaise on their funding policies on Northern Ireland, so that a critical tradition can be maintained in the field of social policy research. Who is to initiate such a move? It would be an appropriate epitaph for the SSRC initiative if the ESRC, rather than preside over the funeral, used the occasion to attempt an exploration of this possibility.

Reference

Darby, J., Dodge, N. and Hepburn, A.C. (1983) *A Register of Economic and Social Research on Northern Ireland 1980–83, with an Introductory Essay*, London: Social Science Research Council.

PART II
RURAL SOCIETY

3 Rural life in Northern Ireland: an overview
R.H. Buchanan

The title of this chapter is taken from a book *Rural Life in Northern Ireland* published in 1947, some forty years ago. Its author, John Mogey, was then a young lecturer in geography at Queen's University, but some years previously he had been employed by the Northern Ireland Council of Social Service to undertake the surveys of rural life upon which his book is based. These surveys were seen by the Council as a necessary preliminary investigation for a wider study of unemployment in Northern Ireland which it had been asked to examine upon its inception in 1938. The Council believed that unemployment in the province as a whole was exacerbated by the precarious state of the rural economy, but it lacked facts: in the words of its then Chairman, the late G.H. Bryson, 'there had been no serious investigation of rural problems for over a century'.[1] Mogey's survey was intended to redress the situation. He was to concentrate on the extent and nature of rural depopulation, and to establish its causes. In particular he was to look at 'the influence of the education system on the outlook of the countryman and the effect of vastly improved transport on his habits'; he was also to consider 'the impact of mechanization on farming and its effects on many rural crafts'.[2] These points are considered in the concluding chapter of the book, but the text is mainly concerned with presenting data on each of the six localities chosen for detailed survey. This includes information on family composition and movement, household income and expenditure, housing conditions and facilities, and farming – in particular the size and composition of farms and their economy. Mogey's work lacks the sophistication of modern household surveys, but as the first systematic investigation of rural social conditions undertaken in any part of Ireland it remains a standard work of great value. This is important in itself, but there are other reasons why it is appropriate to place emphasis on his work in the general context of this conference.

First the survey provides a base-line for the study of change in rural life in Northern Ireland in the second half of the twentieth century. The dates of the survey are especially important in this respect, for in 1941 the province's rural communities had yet to experience the full effects of the wartime drive for increased food production; in many respects the scale and techniques of farming and of farm technology were closer to those of the 1850s than those of the present day. The contemporary photographs which Mogey used as illustrations underline this point: his frontispiece shows oats being hand-cut in a field at Hilltown in County Down, a housewife bakes soda farls on a griddle suspended over an open hearth, a country bus trundles along a deserted road towards a thatched cottage in the foreground. Survey data confirm this sense of a past which today can be seen only in the Ulster Folk and Transport Museum: 93 per cent of houses lacked piped water and a WC; 20 per cent of households surveyed cooked over an open fire; 56 per cent of farms were under 30 acres in size, and gross sales from the farms averaged £545 per annum (for comparison Mogey notes that a village grocery shop had a turnover of about £1000).[3] This is a generalized view of the province's country people in the early 1940s, but it is also more specific, providing details of social and economic life in six localities near Hilltown and Ballygowan in County Down, the Braid Valley and Ballymoney areas of North Antrim, and Lisbellaw and Machen in County Fermanagh.

Unfortunately the raw data of the original Survey do not seem to have survived: at least my enquiries over several years have failed to locate them. But the areas investigated can be identified, and from the sources available it should be possible to reconstruct the sequence of change in these areas during the past four decades, and examine in detail the effects of new policies of social welfare and of innovations in farming on the lives of individual families. The broad outlines of these changes are very familiar : the pattern of farming has been transformed by new techniques of cropping and livestock management, by new methods of marketing and new technology, and by major increases in financial support provided first by national government and later under the European Community. Provision for education, health and housing improved dramatically as a consequence of the welfare legislation of the post-war Labour government, and higher incomes led to substantial improvements in the average standard of living. All this is well known at a general level, but there is less information available on the processes of change at the micro-level in our society. This is where Mogey's survey has a special significance, providing a data-base from which change can be studied and the effects of social and economic policy evaluated in the context of a sample of small-scale rural communities. John Greer among others made this point at the conference sponsored by the Economic and Social Research Council held at Magee in 1983,[4] but so far Colin Thomas is the only person of whom I am aware, to undertake such a study: his recently published essay on County Antrim demonstrates its value.[5]

Studies of this sort can provide results of interest to scholars in several disciplines, including those concerned with development studies. I mention the latter because a recent visit to Brazil confirmed my impression that Northern Ireland in the 1940s bore some resemblance to several countries of the Third World today, for example in the strongly familial organization of its rural society, its pattern of small farms and owner occupancy, its level of technology and welfare provision. Establishing the processes by which our rural society has changed over the past forty years might enable some developing countries to benefit from our experience, not least in the design of appropriate policies for alleviating poverty and improving standards of housing, health-care and welfare.

Mogey's work thus provides a base-line from which to examine the processes of change which have affected our own rural society in the recent past, but it is relevant to us today for another reason. His survey was intended to provide an overview of rural society at a time when the province's economy was in a thoroughly depressed state: it was to provide the information from which the Council of Social Service might proceed to devise new policies for the 're-establishment of a sound rural economy'. In the event the Council did not do so: the war intervened, the economy prospered and in its aftermath, social conditions steadily improved. Today our situation is not unlike that of the early 1940s, in the sense that we too face chronic unemployment and continuing recession. We too need to renew the policies under which we operate, assess their adequacy in meeting present needs and if necessary devise new ones to meet changing conditions. Unlike the Council of Social Service in the 1940s, we do not lack information; but it is mostly available in individual packets, in surveys undertaken for specific purposes by many different agencies and institutions. It needs to be synthesized, to provide the basis for policies which are more comprehensive in approach and implementation. In that sense it is timely to be reminded of Mogey's survey, and the purpose for which it was undertaken.

Before commenting further on the need for a new synthesis, let me refer briefly to the problems we face today, bearing in mind that although my subject is the countryside the distinction between rural and urban is much less evident today than it was forty years ago. Ready access to the media and to modern systems of communication, and a high degree of personal mobility have blurred the edges between town and country. The differences that still exist are based upon distances, greater in the country than in the town, and upon population which in rural areas is less dense and more widely scattered; this in turn increases costs, of transport and in the provision of services. Rural differs from urban in one other respect, its dependence on agriculture. Working farmers now form a minority in the population even of rural areas, but farming and the needs of the farm family still provide a major support for services based in country towns. Hence the livelihood of many people in Northern Ireland depends upon the prosperity of its agricultural industry; and that prosperity is now under threat.

The medium-term prospects for agriculture in Northern Ireland are discussed in detail in the paper contributed by John Spencer and Julie Whittaker (Chapter 4). It is sufficient here to note that recent decisions within the European Community indicate that the level of prosperity enjoyed by farmers in recent decades is unlikely to be sustained: we need to reappraise our present production in the light of current market demands and trends and quite possibly consider new ways of using our land resources. This seems to be essential, given a likely continued downward trend of full-time employment in agriculture, and all that this implies for levels of employment in related occupations.

Agriculture of course is not the only sector of the rural economy facing a reduction in income. Cuts in government spending are currently leading to reductions in employment throughout the public sector, in education, health and welfare; and cuts in expenditure have a knock-on effect upon other services. Closed schools, boarded-up shops, former surgeries converted to private dwellings are visible signs of the change, while spreading pot-holes on country roads and rotting woodwork on public buildings signify less money being spent on routine maintenance. Town and country alike are affected by reductions in public spending, but the consequences may be proportionately more serious in rural areas, undermining the very structure of some communities. For example, cuts in the budget allocation of the province's Forest Service might lead to redundancies in a forest district of West Fermanagh, an area of marginal land with few opportunities for alternative employment. Some families might be forced to leave; and even though the actual numbers may be few, they could be sufficient to jeopardize the future of the local school, reduce the turnover of the local shop and post office to the point where they are no longer commercially viable, and perhaps lead to the withdrawal of the local bus service. Living standards for those who remain would be severely affected, especially for the elderly and infirm. Even those who are more mobile, who own their own transport, would be forced to undertake longer journeys to school, to attend the doctor or to shop, and longer distances take more time and increase costs. The point need not be stressed any further; it is happening throughout these islands and has been the subject of academic research, in Ireland for example, by Mary Cawley.[6] Concern about the situation has also been expressed by many statutory and voluntary bodies, including Rural Voice in Britain and by the Northern Ireland Council for Voluntary Action which is currently sponsoring research in its Rural Action Project.

Of course the level of service provision attained by the mid-1980s is high: it reflects the aspirations and the material prosperity achieved during the more affluent 1960s and early 1970s. Maintenance of this present infrastructure may not be possible with the reduction in public spending which could well continue through the 1990s. To acknowledge that contraction is inevitable is one thing : to establish priorities and to implement cuts is another, and there is as yet little evidence to suggest that we have managed to do so effectively. For example, many decisions on school closures or on the re-grouping of health-care facilities seem to be made as much on the basis of short-term expediency as on long-term planning, and without careful evaluation of public reaction and political response. Planning for contraction it seems, may need different skills and analytical techniques than planning for growth: certainly it represents a very different philosophy from the expansionist view of the 1960s, when many of our decision-makers were trained and gained their early experience.

I have stressed contraction because it is perhaps even more visible in the country than in the town. To be sure, every city has its zones of decay and dereliction, but many areas are simply awaiting redevelopment: urban land is too valuable to lie vacant for long. It is different in the country where deserted cottages, overgrown lanes and abandoned fields may never be reclaimed. Statistical data enable one to pinpoint the areas and periods of decline more accurately: the decline in population revealed in the census, the falling enrolments in country schools, the amalgamation of farms to create larger holdings. In some places contraction has been endemic for decades; in others it is more recent. Certainly there is little uniformity throughout the province, for rural areas differ widely in their capacity for productive farming and in their ability to support population. This point is underlined in Paul Compton's *Census Atlas*,[7] which demonstrates the regional variations present in the province at the time of the 1971 census, using a wide range of data relating to demography, religious affiliation, employment and housing. The value of the *Atlas* can be further enhanced by data derived from household surveys, of the type pioneered in Northern Ireland by Mogey in the 1940s. Of course the Policy and Planning Research Unit at Stormont has been operating a Continuous Household Survey since 1983, and similar surveys have been undertaken by the Housing Executive. It is possible that these data can be used to provide a profile of rural life in Northern Ireland in the late 1980s, as we move into a period of economic retrenchment; if not we need to obtain the information through a new province-wide survey from which a synthesis can be prepared.

Whether the information is used effectively or not is another matter, for often, it seems to me, inadequate use is made of survey data, sometimes even by government departments who themselves have commissioned the work. My comment is based on experience in the field of physical planning, and can be illustrated by reference to a recently published document relating to the Mourne Mountains in County Down, an area of high scenic and conservation value. The published surveys on topics such as derelict buildings and trees 'have been drawn together to provide a data-base upon which policies can be developed and decisions made'; but the same paragraph goes on to state: 'the Department does not wish to make vague proposals which may come to nothing; rather its intention is to seek positive action towards the implementation of proposals.'[8] In fact, no attempt is made to analyse these data, nor to use them as a basis for formulating policies which seek to accommodate development with conservation.

This is unfortunate, for the area concerned does need clear and positive statements on the options for future land use and development if its resources are to be used effectively and for the well-being of its people. It is an upland area, traditionally sheep country with some residual quarrying, and an important centre for outdoor recreation, both for active hill-walkers and mountaineers and for more passive motorists. Hill-farming here is in difficulty and likely to remain so; while prospects for the adjoining lowland farmers are likewise bleak. Their units are small and farming here has been largely a part-time occupation, with alternative employment provided in the building industry, itself now in a depressed state. Alternative uses for local resources need to be found, not least in the considerable potential which exists for outdoor recreation, whose development could generate employment, in remedial work in landscape and conservation, and in the provision of user facilities.

This potential is recognized by several agencies: indeed in planning terms the area is designated both an Area of Outstanding Natural Beauty and an Environmentally Sensitive Area. Yet developments continue, grant-aided and/or approved by government agencies which impair the amenities of the area and are themselves of questionable economic value. Examples include extensive reclamation of marginal land in situations that are harmful to visual amenity, insensitive siting and design of farm buildings and dwellings, and removal of hedgerows and field walls.

Such an area requires an action research programme as suggested by Malcolm Moseley at the 1983 Conference,[9] leading perhaps to proposals for the type of Integrated Rural Development Strategy which has been advocated increasingly in recent years.[10] Such an approach seems essential if new methods of using land resources are to be devised to meet the changing economic and social conditions of the 1980s, and the social infrastructure adapted to meet changing needs. We may also need to experiment with the ways and means of implementing policies based on integrated development, for our existing institutions can be remarkably inflexible when it comes to policy coordination. This may be due to the way responsibilities are fragmented between different agencies, and to the absence of formal channels for effecting communication between them. For example, the area to which I have just referred is administered by three district councils, two education and library boards, one health board, two planning divisions – together with the several departments of central government, their many boards and agencies, and a range of other statutory authorities. Decision-making itself is compartmentalized in a way that real life is not; and decisions themselves are often made at levels within a bureaucracy remote from the locality affected, and largely inaccessible to local opinion. The present political vacuum in Northern Ireland exacerbates the situation, and itself is a factor of great significance in any topic relating to economic and social policy. For decisions are made today by officials without benefit of the public scrutiny and political debate at the provincial tier of administration envisaged when local government was reorganized in 1972. There is little sign that this situation will be resolved in the immediate future, as civil unrest continues and the resumption of 'normal' politics seems very far removed. In these circumstances present procedures for decision-making within Northern Ireland should be reviewed, and academic researchers are best placed to consider and evaluate the options available.

In this overview I have ranged quite widely in my consideration of rural life in Northern Ireland and as befits a non-practitioner in most of the fields I have mentioned, my comments have been presented with the minimum of specific detail: that deficiency will be made good in the papers which follow. I have highlighted several areas in which I think research could be pursued with profit: a re-survey of Mogey's work to provide historical perspective, a more comprehensive social survey of present conditions of rural life, and an application of the concept of Integrated Rural Development in sample areas, for experimentation and evaluation. In several areas I have stressed the relevance of the research for public policy, because I believe the public should benefit more from the results of academic work. That the benefit is perhaps less than it should be is partly a matter of the presentation and marketing of the finished product. Most of the topics I have mentioned are relevant to the work of the Economic and Social Research Council, whose interest in Northern Ireland is much appreciated by those of us who work and live in the province. I need hardly add that we hope that this interest will continue, along with the financial support which is essential for our work.

Notes

1. Mogey, J.M. (1947) *rural Life in Northern Ireland*, Oxford: OUP p. xii.
2. Ibid.
3. Op. cit., Ch. viii.
4. Greer, J.V. In Jess, P.M. et al. (1984) *Planning and Development in Rural Areas*, Belfast: Queen's University, p. 86.
5. Thomas, Colin, (1986) *Rural Landscapes and Communities*, Blackrock: Irish Academic Press, pp. 145-78.
6. Cawley, M.E. (1986) 'Disadvantaged groups and areas: problems of rural service provision'. In Breathnach, P. and Cawley, M.E., 1986, *Change and Development in Rural Ireland*, Maynooth: St Patrick's College, pp. 48-59.
7. Compton, P.A. (1978) *Northern Ireland: A Census Atlas*, Dublin: Gill and Macmillan.
8. Department of Environment for Northern Ireland (1986) *Mourne Area of Outstanding Natural Beauty*, Belfast: HMSO.
9. Jess et al., op. cit., p. 221.
10. Op cit., pp. 103-53. See also Armstrong, J.A. (1986) 'Integrated Development in Western Europe: theory and practice'. In Breathnach, and Cawley, op cit., pp. 69-76.

4 The Northern Ireland agricultural industry: its past development and medium-term prospects
Julie M. Whittaker and John E. Spencer

Agriculture is one of Northern Ireland's most important industries. About 10 per cent of the labour force is directly engaged in agriculture, with more than half officially described as full-time. In the United Kingdom (UK) the figure is under 3 per cent while in the EC-10 some 7.6 per cent of the labour force are engaged in agriculture. Republic of Ireland (RI) figures are not fully comparable but the analogous figure appears to be around 17–20 per cent. Not only is agriculture important in Northern Ireland (NI) but it has not been diminishing significantly over the last ten years and certainly not at anything like the marked extent in RI.

The purpose of the study underlying this chapter was to report on the NI agricultural industry some dozen years after European Community (EC) membership and to provide a compact history taking account of the institutional arrangements and economic forces, primarily of recent years and drawing on a wide variety of sources. It was hoped to assess the fundamental strengths and weaknesses of agriculture in the province, taking account of important economic realities and distinguishing between ephemeral considerations and factors likely to matter in the longer run. It was also hoped to provide an assessment of how agriculture might develop in the province over the next few years. The main analytical approach of the work, apart from its historical component, was to try to assess the direction of the Common Agricultural Policy (CAP), on which the NI industry is assumed to have negligible impact, and then assess the impact of that on NI agriculture, taking account of its economic strengths and weaknesses.

The Common Agricultural Policy (CAP)
The CAP, the main elements of which have been operative since about 1968, has led to the emergence of substantial surpluses in many commodities in the EC, especially some cereals, dairy products and beef.

The high levels of production are supported by price levels determined in annual bargaining sessions between ministers of agriculture. Cheap imports are kept out by a variable levy system and excess domestic supply is typically stored in intervention. These stocks are released on the domestic market in times of shortage or, more usually, released on the international market at a price sufficiently low to enable buyers to be found. The difference between the EC price and the world price constitutes the export refund and the entire cost of storage and refunds is borne by the Community budget. Clearly the extent of the cost is directly influenced not only by the magnitude of the surpluses but also by prices and exchange rates and tends to be higher when world prices are low and when the US dollar is at a low value.

The costs of operating the CAP comprise some 70 per cent of the EC budgetary costs which, since 1980, have been funded by the 'own resource' system whereby 90 per cent of each member state's tariff and levy revenue is contributed along with a limited contribution from VAT. Two points need to be stressed in relation to these arrangements. First, it is entirely clear that there can be grave inequities between member-states in that there is nothing in the mechanism to ensure that a country's receipts need bear any just relationship to its payments. This point has been persistently stressed by the UK since at least 1975. Secondly, there is nothing in the arrangement to guarantee that receipts need be sufficient to match costs, a consideration which has been increasingly recognized since about 1980.

Both of these points are germane in assessing the pressures against the CAP's continuance in anything like its present form. Thus, the UK, while pressing for reform of the budgetary arrangements, has also pressed continuously for reform of the CAP itself – presumably, among other considerations, in order that its total cost decline in case the budgetary arrangements should prove inflexible. And those countries which feel a lack of *'juste retour'* for their budgetary contributions would tend to oppose changes in the VAT limitation necessary to increase the funds required by escalating CAP costs. This force would also generate internal pressure towards reform of the CAP. While these pressures were temporarily reduced by the Fontainebleau Agreement of June 1984 which increased the VAT ceiling and formalized a system of rebates to the UK, the costs of running the CAP have continued to escalate dangerously and the internal pressure for change remains extremely high.

External pressures against the CAP are also extremely important and come from a variety of sources including the USA, other agricultural exporters including Australia, New Zealand, Canada and Argentina, the countries bound by the General Agreement on Tariffs and Trade (GATT) and some less developed countries. In all these cases the major complaint concerns the EC dumping of surplus output on world markets.

The United States, for example, has been a major critic of the CAP, especially perhaps since the early 1980s when large elements of US farming have been in serious difficulties with heavy debts, high interest rates and loss of traditional markets. Against this background agriculture has become probably the single most contentious issue between the EC and the US involving threats of trade warfare.

Agriculture has been, in effect, exempt from GATT rules since the formation of GATT in 1947. Following the Tokyo Round, however, there have been major attempts to bring agriculture within GATT parameters, especially by the US and other traditional agriculture exporters. These attempts have been strenuously opposed by the EC, apparently led by France, fearing that the CAP would be undermined. The net outcome, however, is that agriculture is likely to be on the agenda of the new Round and that the export policy implied by the CAP will at least be seriously threatened.

There is little doubt that these problems of the budget and inequity from within, and of traditional exporters and GATT from without, will have implications for CAP policy, which in turn will have implications for the NI industry. These are considered below, organized by sector.

The dairy industry
Dairying has been the most profitable farming enterprise in the province in recent years, contributing about one quarter of gross output, although it is not suited to all farmlands in the region. Almost 30 per cent of the farms over one ESU have a dairy enterprise, with 8287 registered producers in Northern Ireland in March 1984. This is less than half the number that were registered twenty years ago. Yet while the number of herds has decreased, the average herd size has risen and the total number of dairy cows in the region has also risen until very recently. This is shown in Table 4.1, which compares NI with changes which have occurred in GB and RI. The average herd size in Northern Ireland has tripled since 1960 and is almost double the average herd size in the Irish Republic although it remains small relative to herd size in Great Britain. The growth in the herd size in NI during the 1970s reflects the response to the higher milk prices consequent on EC membership. Production in GB did not respond in the same way,

probably owing to the newly created opportunities for cereals expansion. Cereal growing is not so attractive in the province because of the less suitable climate and small farm structure, and the environment is particularly suited to grassland enterprise.

Table 4.1a Dairy cows at June of each year, ('000 head)

	Great Britain	Northern Ireland	Republic of Ireland
1972	3101	224	1405
1973	3200	236	1445
1974	3153	241	1420
1975	3003	239	1465
1976	2986	242	1500
1977	3020	249	1554
1978	3017	257	1594
1979	3028	264	1624
1980	2958	270	1587
1981	2920	271	1558
1982	2970	280	1590
1983	3039	294	1636
1984	2982	299	1642
1985	2856	294	1633
1986	2849	292	1585

Note: Figures from 1977 onwards include estimates of animals on minor holdings in England and Wales.

Source: *Annual Abstract of Statistics for UK,* 1987.
Dairy Facts and Figures, Federation of UK Milk Marketing Boards, 1976 and 1986.
Irish Statistical Bulletin, CSO, Dublin (various issues).
The number of dairy cows in RI, 1972 and 1973 derived from number of total cows and estimate of beef herd made by B. Kearney, An Foras Taluntais, Dublin as published in 'Agriculture in the Republic of Ireland and Northern Ireland', *Cooperation North* Paper III, 1981.
Annual Review and Outlook of CBF (Irish Livestock and Meat Board) 1986.

Table 4.1b Output of milk (million litres)

	Great Britain	Northern Ireland	Republic of Ireland
1972	12346	866.0	—*
1973	12568	899.8	3328
1974	12217	880.7	3226
1975	12212	921.0	3463
1976	12629	988.6	3729
1977	13350	1056.0	4023
1978	13960	1133.9	4554
1979	13980	1136.3	4655
1980	14012	1170.4	4567
1981	13897	1186.8	4542
1982	14642	1301.3	4952
1983	15026	1415.7	5333
1984	14084	1362.4	5564
1985	13921	1338.5	5655

Source: Annual Abstract of Statistics for UK, 1984 and 1987.
Annual Abstract of Statistics, NI, 1983.
Statistical Review of NI Agriculture, 1985.
Irish Statistical Bulletin, Sept./Dec* 1985, Sept. 1986.

* Means of measuring milk output have changed considerably. No corresponding figure for 1972.

The EC arrangements have as their main aim the achievement by milk producers on average of a target price set for the EC on a delivered dairy basis. The milk target price is supported by the intervention buying of the key dairy products, especially butter and skimmed milk powder, and the internal market is protected by a system of import levies and export refunds. The levies and refunds apply to liquid milk and fresh milk products as well as butter, cheese, etc. in trade with third countries.

This system has generated substantial surplus production. Between 1974, when the EC achieved 100 per cent self-sufficiency in milk and milk products, and 1983, milk deliveries increased by about 2.8 per cent annually compared with an annual EC consumption increase of about 0.5 per cent. The surplus stocks are extremely expensive to store and also expensive to sell on world markets. A co-responsibility levy on producers was introduced in 1977 but this proved inadequate to prevent stocks growing to unmanageable proportions. Accordingly annual quotas were introduced for a five-year period effective from 2 April 1984. Member-state quotas were based on 1981 deliveries (apart from RI, Italy and, later, Spain where the base was 1983). In terms of 1983 wholesale deliveries, the EC total represented a cut of 4.1 per cent, the UK total a 6.2 per cent cut (despite an allocation of 65,000 tonnes extra for Northern Ireland from the EC reserve, an allocation based on an EC acceptance of the argument that dairying was of crucial importance in NI and that there had been substantial growth in output between 1981 and 1983) and the RI total an increase of 4.6 per cent.

The UK quota, which with the others was to be cut by a further 1 per cent the following year, was divided by the UK authorities into regional allocations. The NI allocation has been the subject of prolonged complaint within the province, where it is believed that the 65,000 tonnes allocated by the EC as an extra for NI has been allocated throughout the UK, an allegation denied by the UK authorities. In fact, the NI quota and GB quota were both some 5.8 per cent below total 1983 sales. A further 3 per cent cut was imposed on producers to create a national reserve from which additional quota could be given to (a) producers whose 1983 output was adversely affected by certain exceptional events, and (b) producers who had committed themselves to investments in dairying prior to 1 March 1984. Various outgoers' schemes have also been set up under which quota may be bought and allocated to (c) exceptional hardship cases, and (d) small producers. These schemes have operated regionally in that the reserve and quota released from the outgoers' schemes have in the main only been available to producers in the region whence they originated. Since dairying is so important in the province and alternative opportunities scarce, little quota has become available there while the demands for the categories of extra quota have been correspondingly great. Thus, despite some subsequent transfers from GB, many individual producers possess less quota than their counterparts in similar positions in GB.

NI output was slightly over quota in 1984/85 but no fines were payable by producers as some quota was unused in GB and the EC agreed the nominal transfer of such quota. The following year NI was about one per cent over quota and, as the UK was also over quota, fines were payable. In 1986/87 supplies are likely to be about 1.4 per cent under quota in NI.

The adjustment to quotas has clearly been painful in the province with falls in both the herd size and in milk yields. With announcements in 1986 of further cuts in quota and a tightening of the system at the individual producer level, measures aimed at cutting production by the further 9.5 per cent deemed necessary given the still growing problem of surpluses, it is clear that contraction is inevitable in a major part of NI agriculture.

The beef industry

The output of fat cattle is the most valuable product from the agricultural industry in Northern Ireland. In 1984 it accounted for over 36 per cent of total agricultural output and the proportion was as high as 38 per cent in the late 1970s. Beef is a prominent export from the region accounting for 47 per cent of total agricultural exports in 1984.

The size of the beef herd and the output of fat cattle since 1972 is given in Table 4.2. During the 1960s beef production was encouraged in the UK in various ways including rising guaranteed prices under the UK Deficiency Payment Scheme and the NI beef herd more than trebled between 1960 and 1970. It peaked in 1974 and then followed a long period of decline initiated by the beef crisis of 1973-74 when prices slumped following the energy crisis and full provision for intervention buying was not available. In November 1974 the UK government introduced the Variable Premium Scheme, initially as an emergency measure, but still operative despite EC objections. Under the scheme a variable premium (VP) was payable to bring the average market clearing price up to a predetermined target price (related to the guide price), although an upper limit was placed on the VP. Intervention remains possible although when purchasing beef for intervention the Intervention Board will pay traders only the intervention price less the VP applicable on the date of slaughter.

Under the EC beef and veal regime, the guide price is fixed annually for live animals representing a desired average price within the EC. This price is supported by the intervention price, set at 90 per cent of the guide price, although intervention is restricted in various ways to limit budgetary costs. Intervention buying, bolstered with import levies and export refunds, is the main method of support along with the variable premium scheme in UK and private storage aid.

As with most products under the CAP, official prices are announced in ecus and these are translated into domestic prices by application of the green rates of exchange. Should the green rate differ from the market rate, border taxes and subsidies (MCAs) are applied to prevent arbitrage movements of commodities.

Following the beef crisis described above, the history of the NI beef industry is dominated by interactions with RI, where prices have been maintained through the standard intervention system and which has been a traditional supplier to GB. Owing to differences in green rates, RI prices have tended to be above those in NI from 1974 to 1980 and from mid 1986. These differentials should be sustainable through MCA payments and receipts but in practice smuggling has emerged, from North to South in the periods mentioned. An undesirable effect is the starving of meat plants of supplies with adverse effects on unemployment and this was countered in the earlier period, though not recently, with the introduction of the Meat Industry Employment Scheme (MIES).

Table 4.2a Beef cows at June of each year ('000 head)

	Great Britain	Northern Ireland	Republic of Ireland
1972	1191	285	490
1973	1354	324	651
1974	1548	339	732
1975	1570	327	637
1976	1473	291	547
1977	1400	288	541
1978	1327	262	502
1979	1298	245	484
1980	1254	224	448
1981	1215	205	424
1982	1192	197	429
1983	1164	194	421
1984	1155	196	436
1985	1133	201	446
1986		198	446

Note: Figures from 1977 onwards include estimates of animals on minor holdings in England and Wales.

Source: *Annual Abstract of Statistics for UK,* 1987.
Dairy Facts and Figures, Federation of UK Milk Marketing Boards, 1976 and 1986.
Statistical Review of Northern Ireland Agriculture, 1986.
Irish Statistical Bulletin, CSO, Dublin (various issues).
The number of dairy cows in RI, 1972 and 1973 derived from estimate of beef herd made by B. Kearney, An Foras Taluntais, Dublin, as published in 'Agriculture in the Republic of Ireland and Northern Ireland'. *Cooperation North* Paper III, 1981.
Annual Review and Outlook of CBF (Irish Livestock and Meat Board) 1985 and 1986.

Table 4.2b Output of fat cattle ('000 head)

	Great Britain	Northern Ireland	Republic of Ireland
1972	3064	417	—*
1973	2932	362	1762
1974	3703	479	1830
1975	4281	547	1892
1976	3781	405	1645
1977	3320	527	1825
1978	3337	539	1851
1979	3368	545	1769 .
1980	3556	554	1672
1981	3404	525	1601
1982	3073	463	1583
1983	3332	479	1684
1984	3772	541	1805
1985	3668	550	1764

Source: *Annual Abstract of Statistics for UK,* 1984 and 1987.
Annual Abstract of Statistics, NI, 1983.
Statistical Review of NI Agriculture, 1985.
Irish Statistical Bulletin, Sept./Dec.* 1985, Sept. 1986.
Correspondence with CSO, Dublin.

* CSO, Dublin have revised their definition of fat cattle output with respect to treatment of imports. Consequently there is no comparable figure for 1972.

Under this scheme a headage payment equivalent to the MCA was paid to presenters of cattle (and pigs) for slaughter at Northern meat plants, bringing NI prices up to RI levels and removing the incentives for smuggling.

Other complicated movements of animals, linked with VP and MCA interactions are described in our main report (Whittaker and Spencer, 1986). At times Northern meat plants have benefited, at times Southern meat plants, and much of the movement has been illegal.

In 1984 the VP scheme was weakened, though not abolished, with cuts in the maximum permissible amount payable and with the introduction of clawback on exports. Since meat plants need only pay market price for supplies, generated by producers reacting to that price augmented by VP, the VP acts as an export subsidy.

From 1984, the VP has been 'clawed back' on exported produce, a measure which has been more important in NI than in GB where exporting is much less significant. In the EC as a whole surpluses, as with dairy, have grown to massive proportions. These surpluses are expensive through high storage costs and loss of value through freezing and substantial export refunds are needed to offload them on world markets. Accordingly, as the EC attempts to reduce these stocks, increasingly tight restrictions can be expected on intervention. Private storage aids are likely to become more important as are direct headage payments. The hormone ban, to be effective from 1 January 1988 and likely to be strictly enforced in the UK, will increase costs of beef production, although not just in NI, of course. In the short run some effects of milk quotas are to increase beef supplies as dairy cows are culled, to divert heifers to the beef herd and to increase the proportion of beef bull inseminations. From June 1983 to June 1986 the total number of cows in the EC has declined by over 4 per cent despite an increase of nearly 8 per cent in the beef cow herd. In NI the total number of cows has not declined and the dairy herd has declined little. This small adjustment reflects the lack of alternative opportunities in the province and in the longer run, the local beef industry ought to prove relatively strong with its grass-based production methods. Producers will have to innovate and adapt to the changing and more difficult circumstances, however, especially as there seems little reason for optimism on consumption prospects.

Sheep

Sheep are quite a small enterprise sector within the agricultural industry. In 1984, sheep products of meat and wool together accounted for only 3.5 per cent of total agricultural output in Northern Ireland. A similar situation is recorded for GB and RI, and these are countries which are particularly suited to sheep production, having a climatic advantage in growing grass and considerable area of hills and uplands which are suited to few other agricultural possibilities.

From 1960 to the mid-1970s there was a persistent decline in the sheep flock in NI and, from 1965, in RI. Since 1977 or 1978 expansion has been marked in RI, NI and GB in response to rising producer prices (see Table 4.3). At that time RI gained access to the high price French market and NI benefited by exporting to France via RI. UK pressure for similar access for GB led to the introduction of a common sheepmeat regime in May 1980. The EC is not self-sufficient in sheepmeat and the regime allows for a ewe premium scheme or, if preferred, a variable premium scheme

The Northern Ireland agricultural industry: 45

similar in effect to deficiency payments. Prices are supported by limiting imports through Voluntary Restraint Agreements and there is as yet no need for intervention or export refunds. Basic prices were aligned in four stages up to 1984 and MCAs are not applied. The UK initially opted for the VP scheme even though clawback was payable on exports. Since substantial numbers of live sheep and lambs were soon smuggled from NI into RI to avoid clawback it was decided to change to the ewe premium system in NI from 1982. This has encouraged exporting, mainly liveweight to RI but also deadweight to France. It is clear that the expansion is hazardously dependent on the French market where production is declining and producers militant. EC consumption per capita and in total is static

Table 4.3a Breeding ewes at June of each year ('000 head)

	Great Britain	Northern Ireland	Republic of Ireland
1972	10177	491	1874
1973	10445	475	1872
1974	10719	473	1804
1975	10803	476	1688
1976	10822	477	1603
1977	10758	489	1614
1978	10962	498	1578
1979	11170	513	1577
1980	11639	539	1549
1981	11953	575	1603
1982	12283	626	1648
1983	12640	670	1748
1984	12939	709	1831
1985	13124	769	1999
1986		819	2100

Note: Figures from 1977 onwards include estimates of animals on minor holdings in England and Wales.

Source: *Annual Abstract of Statistics for UK*, 1983 and 1987.
Annual Abstract of Statistics for NI, 1983.
Statistical Review of Northern Ireland Agriculture, 1981 and 1985.
Annual Review and Outlook of the CBF (Irish Livestock and Meat Board) 1985 and 1986.

Table 4.3b Output of fat sheep and lambs ('000 head)

	Great Britain	Northern Ireland	Republic of Ireland
1972	10603	444	—*
1973	11373	386	1716
1974	12567	380	1643
1975	12735	398	1671
1976	12314	356	1461
1977	10956	400	1243
1978	11121	470	1455
1979	11434	450	1447
1980	13697	619	1540
1981	13277	701	1701
1982	13182	712	1679
1983	14353	715	1759
1984	14140	813	1861
1985	14433	855(prov)	2202

Source: *Annual Abstract of Statistics for UK, 1984 and 1987.*
         Annual Abstract of Statistics for NI, 1983.
         Statistical Review of NI Agriculture, 1985.
         Irish Statistical Bulletin, Sept./Dec. 1985, Sept. 1986.
         Correspondence with CSO, Dublin.

* CSO, Dublin have revised their definition of output of fat sheep with respect to treatment of imports. Consequently there is no comparable figure for 1972.

since 1982, despite falling real consumer prices, and New Zealand imports, recently well below the permissible quota, remain threatening, especially if the VP were to be abolished in GB. Abolition would raise market prices and hence imports while consumption would be discouraged. Apparently there is scope for considerable expansion of production in Spain and NI producers will have to pay increasing attention to the quality of carcase. Markets outside the EC will be hard to find, especially in the face of competition from New Zealand.

Pigs, poultry and eggs
The pig and poultry industry has been important in Northern Ireland since pre-war years, an importance all the more notable

because the industry operated for many years within the mixed farming system without a high degree of specialization. Pig production expanded from 1934 onwards, in response to the founding of the Pigs Marketing Board which established assured markets and stabilised prices for pigs. As a result of this growth, by 1936/37 pig and poultry products accounted for 45 per cent gross output. Pig production then declined during the 1940s, since its expansion had depended upon imported grain which became scarce during the war but output recovered when the restrictions to trade were removed. Poultry, however, managed to maintain output during the war years.

It was not until the late 1950s and early 1960s that pig and poultry production became intensive to any extent. This required significant investment in more specialized, large-scale units which resulted in a rise in output. The consequent reduced costs per animal squeezed out many of the small-scale farmyard enterprises. Since the domestic market is small, expansion has involved increasing sales outside the province with most going to the GB market. Consequently NI producer returns are lower than their counterparts on the mainland as Ulster bacon and poultry products shipped to the mainland can only realize the GB market prices, from which shipping costs have to be met. Furthermore, only a small amount of cereals are grown in the province. Thus feed has to be imported and Ulster farmers have to contend with a cost disadvantage compared to mainland producers, even during periods of expansion. This disadvantage, due to transport costs, was fairly negligible until 1973 when imports of grain from North America had to cease. Since then it has been a major factor in the decline of the breeding pig and laying flock populations shown in Tables 4.4 and 4.5. Correspondingly, the contribution of the intensive livestock products to gross output has fallen to around 20 per cent.

The intensive livestock products have only light support under the CAP. The EC is more than self-sufficient in pigmeat and steadily increasing output has more than matched increasing consumption. Pigmeat output has been produced in an increasingly concentrated industry and the fear of the emergence of surpluses suggests that support will remain light. Intervention is possible but has not been used since 1971. The surplus is exported, export refunds are available and imports are restricted. The poultrymeat and eggs sectors have even less support as there is no intervention system, though, again, imports are restricted and export refunds payable. Consumption has grown, quite rapidly in poultrymeat, and the EC is a net exporter of both poultrymeat and eggs.

As mentioned above, 1973 was a turning-point for intensive livestock production in the province, when feed prices rose dramatically owing to a world grain scarcity. While the scarcity was temporary, grain prices never recovered their previous level because the EC support maintained high prices. The level of the threshold price for cereals therefore made it necessary for Northern Ireland to buy Community grain either from England or other EC countries. The cost of transport from cereal-producing areas became a permanent additional cost for Northern Irish intensive livestock producers who, because of their peripheral location within Europe, now had to meet extra transport costs for both their inputs and

Table 4.4a Breeding pigs at June of each year ('000 head)*

	Great Britain	Northern Ireland	Republic of Ireland
1972	851	109	129
1973	903	112	130
1974	819	70	93
1975	744	70	99
1976	807	77	113
1977	762	66	108
1978	764	78	122
1979	770	77	121
1980	759	72	116
1981	771	65	114
1982	794	70	118
1983	786	70	118
1984	737	63	113
1985	764	64	112
1986		62	

Note: Figures from 1977 onwards include estimates of animals on minor holdings in England and Wales.

Source: *Annual Abstract of Statistics for UK,* 1983 and 1987.
Annual Abstract of Statistics for NI, 1983.
Statistical Review of NI Agriculture, 1985.
Irish Statistical Bulletin, various issues.
Correspondence with CSO, Dublin.

*   GB sows, NI sows plus gilts, RI sows plus gilts (plus gilts not yet served 1975–85).

Table 4.4b Output of fat pigs ('000 head)

	Great Britain	Northern Ireland	Republic of Ireland
1972	13650	1754	—*
1973	13567	1516	2143
1974	13785	1489	1670
1975	11991	775	1634
1976	12572	927	1935
1977	13231	963	2055
1978	12773	1014	2279
1979	13474	1243	2272
1980	13341	1283	2170
1981	13718	1147	2173
1982	13964	1126	2236
1983	14838	1151	2270
1984	13790	1148	2150
1985	14114	1148	2025

Source: Annual Abstract of Statistics UK, 1984 and 1987.
Annual Abstract of Statistics, NI, 1983.
Statistical Review of NI Agriculture, 1985.
Irish Statistical Bulletin, Sept./Dec. 1985, Sept. 1986.
Correspondence with CSO, Dublin.

* CSO, Dublin have changed their definition of fat pig output with respect to their treatment of imports. Consequently there is no comparable figure for 1972.

output. These transport costs have been especially significant since the oil price crisis of the early seventies. Although grain, particularly barley, is sometimes available from the Irish Republic, there is apparently only a small economic advantage in buying from this source perhaps because Southern grain traders set prices such that they are little below the price of GB cereals plus shipping costs.

To ameliorate this, the government introduced in mid-1976 a Feed Price Allowance (FPA) scheme, essentially a subsidy to the industry, but this was deemed contrary to EC law and discontinued in 1980. NI producers thus appear to be faced with a serious long-term disadvantage in an industry where feed costs are already a high proportion of total costs. It is important to notice that a reduction in cereal prices would not alleviate NI's serious feed price disadvantage unless prices were reduced right down to world level, and Third Country imports were allowed to enter free of levies. If this were not the case, the feed price disadvantage would only increase both as a proportion of the feed bill (owing to transport costs) and, with reduced product prices, of the sales revenue. That the intensive livestock sector in NI faces serious long-term difficulties is of considerable concern because it is a significant provider of income and employment. In 1983, on farm employment directly dependent on pigs and poultry in Northern Ireland was estimated to be the equivalent of over 4000 full-time jobs, and the

Table 4.5a Laying flock ('000 head)

	Great Britain	Northern Ireland
1972	—*	8444
1973	44489	7277
1974	43556	6368
1975	43241	6118
1976	43465	5620
1977	44427	5189
1978	45661	5324
1979	42949	5171
1980	41418	4594
1981	40125	4348
1982	40513	4279
1983	38721	3759
1984	37165	3408
1985	36360	3178
1986		2933

Note: (i) Republic of Ireland do not publish statistics on laying flock.

(ii) Figures for 1977 onwards include estimates of laying flock on minor holdings in England and Wales.

Source: *Annual Abstract of Statistics for UK, 1985 and 1987.*
Annual Abstract of Statistics for NI, 1983.
Statistical Review of NI Agriculture, 1985.

* Data unavailable.

Table 4.5b Egg production (million dozen)

	Great Britain	Northern Ireland	Republic of Ireland
1972	1089.7	163.3	55.5
1973	1033.3	136.7	55.6
1974	1023.2	127.8	53.5
1975	990.0	123.0	52.9
1976	1037.5	115.5	53.3
1977	1048.6	111.4	50.4
1978	1078.0	114.0	49.8
1979	1073.4	110.6	47.2
1980	1005.1	98.8	42.8
1981	977.5	95.4	49.0
1982	980.8	93.1	46.5
1983	963.4	85.6	48.7
1984	944.1	77.9	51.3
1985	950.9	72.1(prov.)	50.0

Source: Annual Abstract of Statistics UK, 1984 and 1987.
Annual Abstract of Statistics, NI, 1983.
Statistical Review of NI Agriculture, 1985.
Irish Statistical Bulletin, Sept./Dec. 1985, Sept. 1986.
Correspondence with CSO, Dublin.

sector supports a further 5600 jobs within the processing and supplying industries.

In the light of this, it is not surprising that the local pig industry has declined through the 1970s, especially with the local Pigs Marketing Board losing compulsory powers of purchase in 1978. Smuggling has occurred with MCAs payable, and some help was given to the industry with the MIES scheme described above. The industry has a good productivity record and herd sizes are increasing substantially though the industry is not as concentrated as that in RI or GB. It is unfortunate that the industry is biased towards bacon production as the UK market for this, while still large, is declining. As with sheepmeat, care with regard to quality and developments in processing will be essential in the future.

The decline of the egg industry in the province through the 1970s to date has a rather similar story but there is a contrasting record of success in poultrymeat. This success is puzzling as the industry faces, with the rest of the intensive livestock industry, a similar feed cost disadvantage. Certainly, demand factors are involved, as poultry has increased in popularity while eggs have declined, but differences in the structure of production are also surely relevant. Poultry production in the province is extremely highly vertically integrated and concentrated relative to RI or GB. Development has been led by processing firms, particularly one, which encouraged farmers and established contracts with them. Some two-thirds of output is typically exported, most to GB. This success, despite the transport cost problem, may be partly explained by unusual managerial skills but the oligopolistic nature of the local industry is also a likely factor. With the difficult economic circumstances since 1973 felt acutely in NI, demand for cheap poultrymeat has been buoyant there – from 1974 to 1981 consumption doubled compared with a 17 per cent rise in the UK as a whole – and it may have been possible to charge the domestic consumer a higher price, protected by transport costs, than the export market.

Table 4.6a Output of poultrymeat ('000 tonnes)

	Great Britain	Northern Ireland	Republic of Ireland
1972	649.4	29.6	40
1973	634.0	29.0	42
1974	625.1	30.9	38
1975	579.6	32.4	34
1976	618.9	43.1	41
1977	636.5	42.5	44
1978	681.6	44.4	43
1979	702.9	47.1	47
1980	698.3	49.7	50
1981	695.2	51.8	45
1982	755.4	53.6	49
1983	742.2	57.8	49
1984	769.1	55.9	52
1985	—*	56.2	—*

Source: *CAP Monitor*, Agra Europe.
Annual Abstract of Statistics for NI, 1983.
Statistical Review of NI Agriculture, 1985.

* Data unavailable.

Table 4.6b Production of barley ('000 tonnes)

	Great Britain	Northern Ireland	Republic of Ireland
1972	9069	174.6	982
1973	8830	176.6	904
1974	8936	197.0	1040
1975	8323	186.6	1019
1976	7478	172.3	922
1977	10313	217.4	1490
1978	9630	219.9	1568
1979	9350	175.4	1558
1980	10128	197.4	1700
1981	10056	174.4	1670
1982	10757	203.1	1676
1983	9781	199.1	1503
1984	10848	222.0	1770
1985	9578	161.8	1494

Source: Annual Abstract of Statistics for UK, 1984 and 1987.
Annual Abstract of Statistics, NI, 1983.
Statistical Review of NI Agriculture, 1985.
Ministry of Agriculture, NI, 8th Report on Agricultural Statistics of NI.
Department of Agriculture, NI, 9th Report on Agricultural Statistics of NI.
Irish Statistical Bulletin, Sept. 1986.
Correspondence with CSO, Dublin.

While it is tempting to suggest that NI should grow more cereals, especially barley for pig feed, it is doubtful that this makes much economic sense despite occasional ministerial exhortations. The acreage devoted to cereals has fallen by some 20 per cent since 1973 while it rose in GB. Yields in NI are consistently below those in RI or GB and the wet and humid climate, structure of farms, small fields and quality of much of the land make it a high-cost cereal-producing region. Some increased production would not help the intensive livestock producer as the price disadvantage would remain as long as some grain was being imported. While the decline in the pig industry may make it more possible for NI to achieve self-sufficiency at least in barley (and the province approached self-sufficiency of some 70 per cent in 1984) attempts to increase production would be risky, especially with the serious overall surplus in the EC.

Conclusions

In considering the progress of the Northern Irish agriculture industry since 1973, several key phenomena stand out:

(a) the steady 2-3 per cent growth per annum in the dairy cow herd accompanied by steady 5 per cent growth in milk output until the imposition of quotas in 1984;

(b) the rather steady decline from a peak in 1974 to a levelling in 1982–84, at a rate of some 6 per cent, of the beef cow herd;

(c) the steady rise from 1976–77 of the number of breeding ewes at a rate of some 5–6 per cent after broad constancy in the early 1970s;

(d) the sharp decline, at around 40 per cent, in the size of the pig breeding herd between June 1973 and June 1974 with fluctuations around a possibly declining trend since;

(e) the steady decline since 1973 of the poultry laying flock at around 6–7 per cent per annum, accompanied by a similar decline in egg production contrasting with a near doubling of poultrymeat output;

(f) the slow rise to 1978 and slow decline since of the area devoted to barley production; and

(g) the significant fluctuations in real income over the period since 1973 with remarkable low points in 1979 and 1980, especially the latter and the strong rise in agricultural land values in the province, half as strong again as that in England, especially from 1977 to 1979.

The sectors which have experienced the greatest rise in producer prices in NI since 1973 are sheepmeat, beef, milk and broilers, sectors which are important in the province. Given the EC surpluses and tendency for surpluses, policy is likely to be more rigorous in the medium-term future, especially regarding sheepmeat and beef. Milk quotas are likely to remain in operation, and will induce further contraction in the large local dairy sector. The intensive livestock sector will remain under serious pressure for, given EC light support and lack of intervention, low-cost European producers will tend to expand, driving down market prices and putting pressure on the higher-cost producers to leave the industry. And NI producers must, on average, be in the latter category given the feed-cost problem discussed above. The beef sector, however, with grassland management, looks fairly secure in the longer run, despite continued major short-run uncertainties.

The farming community in the EC and elsewhere is going through a difficult period of change and in this, Northern Ireland is no exception. Adjustment will probably change the relative sizes of different sectors within the industry and while the whole may shrink - and there seems little scope for the adoption of new products - it is most likely that agriculture will remain NI's most important industry.

Reference

Whittaker, J.M. and Spencer, J.E. (1986), *The Northern Ireland Agricultural Industry: Its past Developments and Medium Term Prospects*, Department of Economics, The Queens University of Belfast.

Editor's note

For a complementary statistical analysis of agricultural production in Northern Ireland, see T.F. Stainer (1985) *An Analysis of Economic Trends in Northern Ireland Agriculture since 1970*, Belfast, Department of Agriculture.

5 Social and micro-economic processes in the Northern Ireland fishing industry
Reginald Byron and Roy Dilley

The aim of this study is to contribute towards an understanding of the social organization of commercial sea fishing in Northern Ireland, and to account for the remarkable variety of economic strategies pursued by Ulster fishermen through an examination of the micro-processes of social interaction and decision-taking in their fishing activities.

Previous studies of fishing in the province (Hughes, 1970; Butlin, 1981) have taken a formal, largely quantitative approach to the description of the industry's economic structure. While the main outlines have been adequately covered, some significant gaps in the literature concerning the industry still remained. Although these authors present statistics describing a broad range of fishing activities, types of fish caught, kinds of boats and equipment, levels of investment and financial performance, no explanations are suggested for these varying choices or their outcomes; little, if any, data are given on the way fishermen evaluate choices, or what factors or attitudes might influence their choice of a fishing regime. Further, there is no information in these reports that indicates how fish-catching businesses are capitalised, owned or managed, or how labour is recruited. Nevertheless, between 1975 and 1981, more than £12 million was paid out in grants and loans for fishing boats, and further state subventions continue to be made in operating subsidies, the value of harbour improvements and other indirect financial aids to fishermen. As our report (Byron and Dilley, 1986) was eventually to conclude, the gaps in the information available to planners and administrators have had critically important implications in the effectiveness of official policies and public investment programmes in the Northern Irish fishing industry.

This ESRC-sponsored study set out to fill in some of these gaps, and to seek information in five, previously uninvestigated areas: (1) ownership structures, (2) capitalization processes, (3) systems of wage or share distribution, (4) management practices, and (5) labour recruitment patterns. To carry out this research, we sought to complement, rather than to duplicate, the approaches of the earlier studies by adopting contrasting analytical perspectives and methods of data-collection. We adopted a 'grass roots' perspective, seeking qualitative information, using participant observation and informal interviewing as our main means of gathering data. We had reason to believe that, had we adopted more formal methods of approach and interviewing, the answers we would have obtained would have been coloured by the respondents' judgement, based on recent past experience, of what they thought 'the authorities' wanted to hear or what they could be safely told. To minimize this risk, an informal, low-key approach was used. Two years' anthropological-style fieldwork was carried out in Kilkeel, County Down, the largest fishing port in the province. In taking a 'grass-roots' view, our study attempted to describe the world of fishing as the fishermen themselves saw it, and to explain their decisions in terms of the perceptions to which they attached significance. We sought, then, to describe these aspects of organization with reference to the choices made by individual fishermen in the light of their personal circumstances, rather than as responses to broader economic forces; we took the view that social factors are not the simple derivatives of economic forces nor vice versa – rather, we regarded both as in a process of interplay, producing complex patterns of interaction.

The Kilkeel fishing fleet

In 1984, the Kilkeel fishing fleet comprised 84 boats of four principal types. Those less than 60 feet in length are mainly 'prawn' boats which are used in bottom-trawling for nephrops, but which may also take white fish as a byproduct. Additionally, a number of boats of approximately 60–80 feet in length, powered by somewhat more powerful engines, are used to catch a variety of species of fish as well as nephrops. These two types of boat make up a majority of the fleet, around 60 vessels. A third type, mid-water trawlers, are usually over 70 feet in length, powered by yet larger engines, and are used chiefly to fish for migratory species such as cod and herring, depending on the time of year. The last category of vessels is made up of purse-seiners, of which there are three in the fleet, each over 100 feet in length; while these boats can also trawl for white fish and cod, they are used principally in catching herring and mackerel. There is a close relationship between the size of the boat and the level of capital investment required: prawn fishing is the cheapest form of fish-catching venture, and purse-seining is the most expensive. The size of the boat is also a measure of its seaworthiness and cargo capacity, and so, indirectly, of its dependence upon a local port: prawn boats are best suited to work in local waters, while boats in the 60–70 foot range may work farther offshore and have sufficient capacity to take their week's catch to be sold in Whitehaven or another Irish Sea port. Purse-seiners, the largest class of fishing boat, may make trips weeks in duration on distant fishing grounds, and sell their catch at any port in the British Isles, wherever the highest prices can be obtained.

The share system

Fishermen do not receive a weekly set wage, but are paid according to a share system which allocates the vessel's income across certain conventional categories of expense. Against the gross income received from the sale of fish are deducted the boat's running expenses and certain fixed expenses such as the rental of electronic equipment. The remainder is then divided into two equal parts: one is called the 'boat share', which goes to the owner of the vessel for its upkeep and his profit, if any; and the other part is called the 'crew share', which is equally divided among the members of the crew as payment for their labour. All the boats in the Kilkeel fleet operate on this basis, and there is little variation in the way these shares are reckoned. Accounts are kept on a weekly basis, when the skipper 'settles up' with his crew. Payments to crewmen are made on a Friday or Saturday, after a book-keeper, the skipper's wife or the skipper himself has 'squared up' the books.

The income from the sale of the week's catches is received from the boat's agent or auctioneer, who deducts an agreed sum to cover his commission (5 per cent), landing dues to be paid to the harbour authority (1 per cent), and the Producers' Organization levy (0.5 per cent). Some skippers also pay for their ice and harbour dues through their auctioneer, thus bringing the total deductions to around 10 per cent. On receiving the net sum from the auctioneer, the boat's book-keeper then calculates the amounts needed to meet the running costs: these include hire charges on the Decca Navigator, radar, radiotelephone, VHF radio, echo sounders, sonar, boat insurance and lubricating oil. Next are deducted fuel oil, stores and provisions for the week, cooking gas, National Insurance contributions and possibly ice, customs charges and harbour dues. The net sum remaining after these deductions are made is then divided into two equal parts, the boat share and the crew share. Each crewman, including the skipper, receives an equal proportion of the crew share. The owner receives the boat share, from which he must meet the costs of maintaining the vessel and its nets and gear, as well as mortgage repayments, if any. If, after the owner has met these expenses, there is any surplus on this account, he may choose either to reinvest it or to treat it as profit.

An example of the average weekly earnings of a typical boat taken over a period of a year illustrates how the system works:

Gross earnings, per week	£3000
Running expenses	1000
Net earnings	2000
Crew share	1000
Six men each receive	166
Boat share	1000
Owner's costs	850
Owner's profit	150

In this case, the owner of the boat was also the skipper, so he received a total of £316 including his crew share, compared with £166 per week earned by his crewmen.

Boat ownership
Historically, the role of local land-based investors has been important in the establishment of fishing enterprises. Groups of investors either included a skipper as a joint-owner of the boat, or a skipper was hired to operate the vessel. Since the end of the Second World War, with the introduction of government grant and loan schemes for the industry, fishermen have become less reliant upon shore-based investors. Government aid programmes, banks and other financial institutions have come to provide the ever-increasing amounts of capital needed to purchase modern fishing vessels. Local investors are still important, however, in providing start-up capital in a partnership with a young skipper. None the less, patterns of ownership and the expectations of the fishing community have changed over this period. Today, boat-owning partnerships with local businessmen are a temporary expedient in the process of acquiring sufficient capital to buy a boat, and a means to an end in the achievement of financial and managerial autonomy on the part of the skipper-fisherman. The present-day pattern of ownership in the fleet reflects this: 54 vessels are solely owned by their skippers, 21 are held in partnership with a local investor, and nine boats are solely owned by non-fishermen who hire skippers to operate them.

Government financial aid programmes have not, then, totally supplanted the local land-based investor, since these schemes usually provide capital to established or recognized skippers only. Local investors, in combination with banks and finance houses, still have a role in helping young skippers to purchase their first boat. Established skippers, however, can now more easily achieve their goal of independence from local land-based capital and develop the size of their fishing ventures through the take-up of government and institutional finance. Government loans to the industry were discontinued in 1981, since when banks and other financial institutions have become crucially important as sources of investment capital for fishermen. Yet there are significant differences between skippers in their approach to borrowing and investment, and this factor can be used to make an initial distinction between types of fishing enterprise or categories of entrepreneurship.

These categories derive from local distinctions made by the fishermen themselves. The first is a conservative or 'canny' fisherman: one who is disinclined to borrow capital to acquire a boat and tries to keep his debts to a minimum. He is willing, however, to form partnerships with land-based investors since this arrangement does not involve direct money-lending. This relationship is seen more as a kind of patronage in which the skipper can convert labour into captial investment by gradually buying out his partner's stake over a period of time; eventually,. the skipper aims to become the sole owner of his boat. The second type is a petty or 'easy-going' fisherman. He does not avoid borrowing as a matter of policy, but borrows only that which is minimally necessary to purchase a vessel which will provide a reasonable level of income for him, without having to extend himself to meet capital repayments. The third type, a determined fishermen or 'a goer', is essentially a steady, hard-working skipper. His relatively limited aspirations can be met by application and graft, and he is likely to have ·a moderate mortgage on a reasonably modern and well-equipped vessel. Finally, 'go-ahead' or high-risk-taking skippers are entrepreneurs who have invested large amounts of their own savings and borrowed capital in a vessel. They are highly motivated, independent and autonomous, and consequently try to avoid partnerships with land-based investors, even at an early stage in their careers.

Boat management

Styles of boat management vary across these four categories of fishing entrepreneurship, and the recruitment of crews is one issue that can be taken to illustrate these differences. For example, one of the ideals of kinship obligations is to offer economic favours to kinsmen, a category of persons seen to extend to the degree of second cousins. However, many skippers resist giving jobs to them, and this is related to the problems that are associated with hiring and firing unsuitable deckhands. One's kinsmen or 'friends', as they are known locally, are often close social acquaintances, and the social consequences of firing a relative who proves unsuitable are far greater than the sense of offence felt by kinsmen who are not offered jobs in the first place. Some skippers may well refuse to employ a kinsman on their own boats, but they would certainly try to use their influence to find a kinsman a job on another skipper's boat.

There are, however, differing attitudes and practices concerning the employment of kinsmen among the various types of fishermen. For example, determined and 'go-ahead' skippers, who have clear ideas about developing their fishing enterprises and advancing their position in the fleet, adopt a mode of recruitment that does not leave them unnecessarily constrained by the social consequences of hiring and firing deckhands, particularly kinsmen, in order to build an effective and efficient body of crewmen. By contrast, the less ambitious petty fisherman, or even more typically the conservative or 'canny' skipper, is more willing than his more ambitious fellow skippers to admit kinsmen to his crew, even if they are less than ideally competent deckhands, since his crew is not seen as the means of his own promotion within the fleet.

Types of boat and modes of organization

It is among the class of small bottom-trawlers, the 'prawn' boats, that most of the conservative fishermen are to be found. Also included in this class are younger skippers who are getting a start in the industry. This type of vessel is ideal for a 'canny' or conservative skipper, since it requires a relatively small investment of capital, its running costs are modest, and fishing for sedentary nephrops involves less risk than fishing for migratory species. Profits from the enterprise are kept within largely family-based crews and are not dispersed among strangers or non-kin.

Skippers of dual-purpose vessels are of mixed types with varying attitudes to work, investment and management. These vessels are within the reach of conservative and petty fishermen, but the majority are operated by 'goers' or determined skippers. It is among the last category that commitments to family are most sharply separated from the fishing venture. These skippers rarely employ kinsmen, thus leaving them unencumbered by the conflicting interests of kinship obligations and the personal ambitions of the owner-skipper. This is the largest sector of the fleet and competition for limited stocks is greatest within it. Thus, many of these skippers adopt a restricted crew recruitment policy and a competitive business outlook.

Mid-water trawling demands more capital investment than either of the two classes of vessel mentioned above, as the boats require more powerful engines, sophisticated electronic equipment and more elaborate nets and net-handling systems. These skippers, many of whom have achieved this position by taking out large loans, represent a small group for whom the economic risks are high but the rewards are potentially great. Crew recruitment and boat management at this level are much the same as for the 'goer' skipper operating a dual-purpose boat.

The three largest and most sophisticated vessels in the fleet are the purse-seiners, and these boats represent the height of achievement in the locality. Their skippers are high-risk-taking entrepreneurs, each of whom has invested over £1 million in his boat. While the running costs of these boats are extremely high, their earnings are proportionately large. These skippers have shunned land-based partnerships and value their own independence. They have steered clear of involvement with kinsmen in their fishing enterprises throughout their careers, though once they achieved this ultimate level of boat ownership, their style of management has in some respects become more relaxed. These skippers have changed their mode of crew recruitment from one characteristic of a 'go-ahead' fisherman during the period in which they were becoming established, to one in which some immediate kinsmen, usually affines, are given employment. This is not because familial obligations are felt to be less of a constraint upon their managerial autonomy, but that the employment of these kinsmen represents a token of largesse on the part of the skipper in recognition of his own privileged status.

Fishing and religious affiliation
Many fishermen say that religious affiliation is unimportant within the fishing industry, but this is true only to the extent that fishing provides common ground for cooperation at sea and on the quayside, and gives Catholic and Protestant fishermen common topics of conversation. Religious affiliation in fact often determines a fisherman's choice of local services and suppliers, from his patronage of grocers' stores and chandleries to net-menders, boat repairers and accountants. Fellow co-religionists seek out each other's patronage and custom, so that a line of religious division can be traced through the fleet, as in most of the community's life.

Religious affiliation also often affects a skipper's crew recruitment policy and his access to investment capital. The relative paucity of sources of start-up capital from the small number of local Catholic-owned businesses and the lower rate of access to government finance schemes prior to 1973 are two factors that have militated against the progress of Catholic skippers through the fleet at the same pace as their Protestant counterparts. The last ten years or so have seen a marked increase in the number of Catholic-owned boats in the fleet, now representing about one-third of all vessels.

Thus, the differences in the position of skipper-owners of various religious affiliations within the fleet are connected with the ease of access to economic resources, and not to any assumed relationship between business morality and religious belief. The only connection of this sort that can be made is with members of certain Protestant sects who avoid investing large sums of borrowed money in a fishing vessel because of notions of morality related to moneylending.

Policy implications

Although this study did not set out, as it was originally conceived, to make specific policy recommendations, but only to provide an ethnographic account of certain features of local-level economic and social organization, in the event a number of policy-related issues emerged from the analysis of the data. These are outlined in a recent report (Byron and Dilley, 1986). Limitations of space here permit just two representative issues to be highlighted: these concern the way fishing boats are owned, and the way that government loan programmes have worked.

Most skippers aspire to the sole ownership of their boat, as mentioned earlier. Sole ownership has many attractions. Financially, the skipper is entitled to keep all the profits, as well as paying himself wages. How he spends this money, whether for reinvestment or personal consumption, is entirely his own affair. Although he may consult his crew about certain matters, he is under no obligation to do so and he has complete autonomy in the management of his business. He can hire and fire at will, and his leadership cannot be disputed by any other member of the crew. As the skipper is owner of the boat and leader of the crew, the success of his boat will be identified with him personally. If his boat does well, he will gain the respect of the community and his family will enhance their social standing.

By contrast, ordinary crewmen – men who are not skippers – on the less successful boats are forced to decide, virtually on a daily basis, whether it is more worthwhile to go fishing or to stay ashore to collect the dole. When it is considered that there is no 40-hour week in fishing and that 16-hour working days and 60- to 80-hour weeks are not uncommon, then the comparison between the possible hourly return for a day's or a week's fishing and the standard rate of state benefit sometimes makes the dole a more attractive option. While successful owner-skippers may create wealth through entrepreneurship, this wealth is not distributed among the other members of the crew, as it is in many other fishing communities in the North Atlantic region. In Kilkeel, the normal pattern is one of a sole owner and a crew of casually-employed hired men, but this is not at all typical of the way boats are owned in other fishing communities in Britain and Northern Europe. In many other fishing ports, boats are owned in partnerships of three to six working fishermen, one of whom will be the skipper. In this system, the earnings of the boat are much more evenly distributed among the co-owners; each has a share in the profits to augment his basic wages. For a given net income to the boat, a co-owning crewman will have substantially higher earnings (by as much as 100 per cent) than a crewman who, as in Kilkeel, does not own a share in the boat. In Kilkeel, the result of the practice of sole ownership is that there are considerable numbers of men in very poorly paid and extremely insecure employment. For this, as well as a number of connected reasons, we have recommended that the development of partnerships of fisherman-owners – such as those commonly found elsewhere – should be encouraged, with the aim eventually of supplanting the sole ownership by skippers of boats whose purchase is financed from public funds.

Between the mid-1970s and the early 1980s, large amounts of public money were invested in fishing boats in Kilkeel. The distribution of these grants and loans appears to have been rather imbalanced, and seems to have had the effect of acting against the best interests of the local fishing industry. The grant and loan programmes during these years were aimed at stimulating the building of new boats. Much less attractive aid (and sometimes none at all, depending on the age of the boat) was offered for improvements to existing boats, and no aid whatever was available for the purchase of secondhand boats. However, the escalating costs of purchasing a new fishing vessel since the early 1970s have placed huge financial burdens on their owners, which may have acted to deter all but the most optimistic, determined or imprudent fishermen.

The emphasis on building new boats, to the virtual exclusion of all else in recent programmes, makes little sense from the fisherman's point of view. Since this emphasis on the purchase of new boats has been at the expense of any coherent policy of up-grading older boats, it has had the effect of penalizing the majority of fishermen: those who wished to pursue reasonably prudent business practices and who did not wish to take on financial commitments with which they could not easily cope. A number of those fishermen who did buy new boats were otherwise prudent businessmen forced to risk high levels of investment rather than buy secondhand or up-date an older boat, and several have been bankrupted as a result.

This situation has come about by the fact that, on the one hand, fishermen were being given big loans to buy new boats by one governmental agency, while on the other hand restrictive quotas and closed seasons were being introduced increasingly by different agencies. This virtually guaranteed that these new boats could not be made to pay. Governmental agencies were thus acting at cross-purposes and the fishermen who bought new boats were trapped in a bureaucratic vice, squeezed until they were forced to choose between flouting the fishery regulations or defaulting on their loans.

Fishermen are sometimes blamed by the policy-makers for the ills of the industry: they are said to be short-sighted in their investment strategies and reluctant to change their ways, so hindering the government's efforts to promote a more efficient fishing industry. For their part, the fishermen claim that they are being pilloried for the mistakes of the policy-makers. Seen from the fishermen's point of view, the rationale of fisheries policy is not always readily comprehensible, and changes in policy have been frequent over the last fifteen years, occurring unpredictably and without any apparent coordination between the agencies involved. Fishermen are, quite simply, unable to plan ahead because these agencies seem to have so few fixed priorities or coordinated plans for the development of the industry. Without more effective coordination of governmental policies and coherent plans for the future in the management of investment and fish stocks, the industry can operate only on short-term planning horizons from one year to the next, and fishermen who wish to make long-term investments must continue to trust more to providence than to planning.

Reference
Byron, R.F. and R.M. Dilley, (1986) *Ulster Fishermen: Social Bases of Economic Strategy*. Research report to the ESRC, grant A0 5252023.

PART III
ECONOMIC
PERSPECTIVES

6   Prospects for the Northern Ireland economy: the role of economic research
Graham Gudgin

It is well known that Northern Ireland possesses some of the most serious and long-established economic problems of any region of the United Kingdom. High unemployment, out-migration and low family incomes are in each case more serious problems in Northern Ireland than in other regions. At the same time it is much less well known that economic growth in the province has been above the national average over the last quarter century. Indeed, for much of that period Northern Ireland was the fastest-growing UK region other than East Anglia and the South-West both of which gained from the huge decentralization of activity out of London.

This apparent paradox of relatively rapid growth alongside serious social problems is due to the fast natural increase of population in Northern Ireland. Growth of employment would need to be very rapid by UK standards, if all of the natural increase in the labour force were to be fully occupied within the boundaries of Northern Ireland. Although economic growth has until recently been rapid by United Kingdom standards, the UK rate of growth has itself been relatively low. The essence of the economic problem of Northern Ireland is that is an economy with a rapidly growing labour force tied to a slow-growing national economy. Slow growth in the national economy after 1974 has had serious implications for Northern Ireland. Equally worrying is the fact that recovery in the national economy since 1982 has largely excluded Northern Ireland.

If we accept that for the foreseeable future the labour force expansion will continue to be relatively rapid, notwithstanding a falling birth-rate, then any solutions to the social problems can be reduced to two categories. Either the UK national economy increases its long-term rate of growth with Northern Ireland eventually being pulled along in the train of national expansion, or the local economy somehow detaches itself from the constraints of the national economy and grows much faster. This in turn poses three questions relevant to the future of the Northern Ireland economy. Will the trend rate of national growth improve substantially? If it does, will Northern Ireland share proportionately in the improvement? It it does not, how can Northern Ireland achieve faster growth while the national economy is growing too slowly ever to result in full employment in Northern Ireland?

On the first question there are some signs that national growth has improved since the early 1980s. However the experience has been too short to be able to predict whether this is any more than a lengthy recovery from the deepest industrial recession this century. A deteriorating balance of trade since 1982 suggests recovery rather than improvement in the long-term trend rate of growth. While there are unmistakable signs of a major improvement in national industrial competitiveness, it would appear that these are sufficient only to maintain the shrunken UK share of world trade but not to reverse the long-established decline in this share. If the UK is able to maintain its share of trade, growth will depend directly on expansion of the world economy. As yet there are no signs of the coordinated expansion necessary to return to the pre-1974 'golden age of growth' in the industrialized economies. However, any future return to a faster trend rate of growth in the world as a whole may be more fully reflected in UK expansion than has been the case in the forty years prior to 1980.

A faster-growing national economy could be expected to improve Northern Ireland's economic position in three ways. There would be an increased demand for the products of Northern Ireland industry, agriculture, and perhaps less obviously its services. Secondly, physical congestion and labour shortages particularly in the South-East would ease the task of attracting mobile businesses to Northern Ireland. Finally, and perhaps most importantly, improved job opportunities in Great Britain and elsewhere would lead to a faster flow of out-migrants. In the 1950s and 1960s almost all of the increase in excess supply of labour was able to migrate. As a consequence unemployment did not increase, although it did remain high by national standards. Since then reduced employment opportunities in Great Britain have meant that a proportion of potential migrants have not been able to leave, and unemployment has risen faster than in Great Britain.

If, as it seems likely, national growth is to remain too sluggish to achieve anything close to full employment in Northern Ireland for the foreseeable future then the local economy must increase its own rate of expansion. This will not be easy since the past quarter-century rapid growth in Northern Ireland has depended heavily on government intervention. During the 1960s government controls and incentives led to large-scale inward investment in manufacturing industry. Low levels of industrial investment in the UK, widespread national unemployment and the political troubles have all caused inward investment to fall to a low level, and the experience of the 1960s is not likely to be repeated. In the 1970s rapid growth was attained through the transfer of a rising share of UK public expenditure to Northern Ireland. Now that public service provision appears to be broadly on a par with Great Britain, taking into account higher needs within the province, it is difficult to imagine any large scope for a future pre-emption of a greater share of public resources.

This leaves the locally-based private sector, albeit with the possibility of continued or even increased public sector assistance. The need is to improve the competitiveness of the Northern Ireland private sector economy so that it can increase its market share in slow-growing national and world economies. The general aim must inevitably involve an increase in the competitiveness of the local economy, in the sense of increasing its capacity to earn income from external markets. To this we might also add the aim of import-substitution, although in a very small, and inevitably highly open economy, the scope for growth through import substitution will be limited. In any case those policies which tend to increase competitiveness will be as relevant to the domestic market as to external markets. In the past, economic growth in Northern Ireland has depended on a redistribution of national activity. Further redistribution looks unlikely and the private sector within the province must become increasingly competitive if the rate of economic growth is to rise significantly.

In this chapter a number of suggestions are made on ways in which the economics profession might contribute to the study of competitiveness in ways which are helpful to policy formulation. Before doing so the problems and recent performance of the Northern Ireland economy are briefly reviewed.

Social problems of the Northern Ireland economy

Each of the social problems alluded to at the beginning of this chapter can be traced to a shortfall of jobs relative to a rapidly growing labour force. Employment shortfalls manifest themselves not only in unemployment, which has typically been 4–6 per cent above the UK average, but also in out-migration and low rate of participation of the working-age population within the labour force. In the fourteen years between 1965 and 1979, over 100,000 more people of working age left Northern Ireland than entered, giving a net loss of 12 per cent of the working age population. In the more depressed conditions of the following seven years up to 1986, the net annual outflow has been lower but has nevertheless led to the loss of another 30,000 people. The total of net out-migrants since 1965 is almost identical to the current number of registered unemployed. In the absence of out-migration the unemployment rate might have risen by one third to around 24 per cent.[1]

Much of the true unemployment in regions with slack labour markets is likely to be concealed. Regions with high registered unemployment tend also to have low participation rates. Many people of working age, especially women, neither work nor register as unemployed. For some people this may represent a conscious choice not to seek work. However the geographical coincidence of low participation with high unemployment suggests that many people are potential workers, discouraged from seeking work by the knowledge that little is available. In 1986 the Northern Ireland participation rate was 73 per cent, second lowest to that in Wales, 5 percentage points below the UK average, and 10.6 percentage points below that in the South-East. If these apparently discouraged workers chose to register as unemployed then the unemployment rate might rise by a futher 5 to 10 percentage points. In the absence of both out-migration and low participation registered unemployment in Northern Ireland might be between 30 and 35 per cent of the labour force instead of the current 18 per cent.

Table 6.1 Employment accounts comparing Northern Ireland and the United Kingdom, 1971–86

	Northern Ireland	United Kingdom
Ex-ante change in labour force[2] *due to:*		
natural increase	18.6	8.2
change in participation	11.3	7.0
less		
Change in employment		
full-time	–5.5	–4.6
part-time	5.5	5.1
equals		
Change in employment shortfall	29.9	14.7
of which:		
Rise in jobs on government schemes	3.1	3.4
Net out-migration	12.2	1.3
Rise in registered unemployment	14.6	10.0
Memo item: Unemployment 1986	18.6	11.8

The salient characteristics of this economic demography are set out in Table 6.1 which describes changes in the supply and demand for jobs in the period since 1971. The table shows the change in employment shortfall with the latter defined as the difference between *ex ante* changes in labour and changes in employment. The change in employment shortfall measures the additional employment necessary to prevent a rise from base year unemployment given the natural increase in labour force together with increases in participation. *Ex ante* changes in labour force are those changes which would have occurred in the absence of net migration losses of working-age people. They consist of natural increase in working-age population plus changes in the proportion of working-age people who decide to enter the labour force. The difference between this *ex ante* labour force and the actual labour force consists of working-age migrants who would have entered in the labour force had they remained in Northern Ireland.

Compared with the national average, the labour force increased by almost 30 per cent over the period compared with half that rate in the UK. Most of the difference was due to a higher rate of natural increase, but in the 1970s the rapid expansion of public sector employment, particularly in health and education, led to a rise in female employment, This in turn led to an increase in participation in the labour force as many women, who would otherwise have been neither employed nor registered as unemployed, joined the labour force.

Employment growth in Northern Ireland was rapid until 1979, but severe contraction has occurred since then. Taking the period 1971–86 as a whole, growth was negligible, as it was also in the United Kingdom as a whole. A decline in full-time jobs, consisting largely of male jobs, was offset by a similar expansion of part-time jobs mostly taken by women. Rapid increase in the labour force without expansion in employment has led to a large rise in the employment shortfall. In Northern Ireland the shortfall has been the largest of any UK region at double the national average.

It has been a general rule across UK regions in recent decades that migration is equivalent to some 80–90 per cent of the excess of a region's employment shortfall over the average shortfall in the nation. Northern Ireland fits into this generalization since the employment shortfall was 15 per cent above that in the UK as a whole, while recorded out-migration was 12 per cent. However net migration failed to absorb the entire local excess in the employment shortfall, and unemployment rose by more than the UK average (Table 6.1).

Any gap in employment opportunities between regions is reflected largely in migration and not in a relatively large rise in unemployment. What is generally true for all regions holds specifically for Northern Ireland, and most of the impact of the high employment shortfall in Northern Ireland is expressed in the high rate of out-migration. It might be expected that differences between regions in employment shortfall might lead to a commensurate widening in unemployment rates. While some widening does occur this is usually less important than the migration flows. In Northern Ireland the excess employment shortfall over the UK shortfall was 15.2 per cent. Only 4.6 per cent of this was absorbed by a widening unemployment gap.

Unemployment has none the less risen greatly since its postwar low in 1973. Most of this rise reflects the national and international recession which has affected the UK, and all of Western Europe, since 1974. Unemployment has risen more in Northern Ireland than in the UK, or Western Europe, not primarily because employment growth has been less than elsewhere but because out-migration has been too low relative to the fast growth in the labour force. The relatively low rate of net out-migration itself reflects the lack of job opportunities in Great Britain and elsewhere during a period of sustained recession. Migrants must compete for jobs with locals in the destination regions, and this competition has become more difficult.

Low per capita, or family, incomes in Northern Ireland are primarily a reflection of the labour market characteristics outlined above. Average earnings for men are currently around 10 per cent below the UK average. For women there is less difference between Northern Ireland and the national average. The fact that *per capita pre-tax incomes* are 20 per cent below the national average is due to:

(i)   the higher level of unemployment, as the unemployed typically have incomes of half of those in work,
(ii) the low rate of participation, leading to a high ratio of adult dependants to wage-earners in the population,
(iii) larger average family size in Northern Ireland than in Great Britain, giving a high ratio of young dependants.

In short, a lower proportion of the population have incomes from employment and these incomes are shared across a larger number of dependants. Overall there are 2.8 people in Northern Ireland for every one at work. The comparable figure for Great Britain in 2.3. Also the magnitude of income redistribution through the tax and benefits system is relatively small. Taking all of these factors into account, disposable after-tax income per capita is 16 per cent below the national average.

Employment growth over two decades

In the period of national full-employment up to 1973, Northern Ireland was the fastest growing UK region in terms of employment, except for those regions flanking the South-East of England. Table 6.2 shows that the better performance in those years occurred notably in government services, but also in each of the production sectors, including construction. In manufacturing, the province gained from the steady stream of inward investment referred to above. On average some 6000 new jobs were created each year by these companies. Government involvement in job-creation was also important in the construction and public utilities sectors, and of course in government services.

Since 1973 the production sectors have all lost jobs more rapidly in Northern Ireland than in the UK as a whole. After 1973 Northern Ireland's employment continued to outpace the UK average but for different reasons. Manufacturing jobs fell faster than in Great Britain as the effectiveness of government incentives declined. A lower level of investment nationally, has provided fewer mobile projects, while the virtual universality of high unemployment has made inoperable the former policy of locational controls on investment. Growth was maintained because employment in government services rose faster under direct rule from Westminster, than was the case in Great Britain. This in turn provided many jobs for women and increased family incomes leading to higher spending on local private services.

During 1980s the relative position of Northern Ireland has worsened considerably. Although employment has continued to rise in both the public and private services sectors, this growth has been slower than in Great Britain. The period in which Northern Ireland's share of UK government spending steadily increased came to an end in 1979 as standards of public service provision attained national levels. The consequent ending of large scale public construction programmes led to a larger fall in construction jobs in the province than in Great Britain. The most important decline was however in manufacturing where 30 per cent of employees lost their jobs in six years. The rate of loss was only slightly greater than the national average despite the closure of a large proportion of the factories which had come into Northern Ireland as inward investment from the 1950s onwards. Many of these firms had been well established in the province, but were unable to survive the consequences of severe over-capacity in the multinational and multi-regional companies of which they formed part.

Table 6.2 Employment growth, 1965–86 (per cent per annum)

	1965–73		1973–79		1979–86	
	NI	UK	NI	UK	NI	UK
Agriculture	–1.5	–3.2	–1.9	–1.5	–1.4	–1.0
Manufacturing	–0.6	–1.1	–2.4	–1.3	–4.7	–4.2
Construction	0.4	0.0	–1.3	–1.7	–5.0	–0.8
Public utilities	0.6	–2.4	2.3	0.2	–1.9	–2.5
Transport, communication	–1.6	–0.7	–1.1	0.0	–1.6	–1.2
Private services	–1.6	0.3	4.0	1.3	1.1	2.4
Government services	5.9	3.5	3.7	1.9	0.2	0.2
TOTAL:	0.6	–0.1	1.0	0.2	–1.2	–0.4

Sources: Dept of Economic Development, NI.
Dept of Employment, GB.
Note: figures include self-employed.

After two decades of large-scale public intervention, Northern Ireland has an economy more dominated by the public sector than any other region in the UK (Table 6.3). Following recent privatization around 42 per cent of employment is within the public sector. The private sector is correspondingly small. Manufacturing now employs only one in six people, as low a proportion as the South-East of England where financial and other services provide alternative bases for the regional economy. While the smallness of the manufacturing sector has shielded Northern Ireland from some of the worst effects of industrial recession it also provides only a limited basis for any industrial recovery.

A small manufacturing sector does not, of course, matter much if other activities are able to earn income from the outside world. To some extent this role is filled by agriculture in Northern Ireland. Including the self-employed, agriculture, forestry, and fishing employ 8 per cent of the workforce, a proportion which is half as high again as that in the most rural regions in Great Britain. Private services in contrast contribute relatively little to the potential for the local economy to generate income from outside. In this respect Northern Ireland resembles the Midlands regions of England, and like them has a low proportion of jobs in private services. Private services in Northern Ireland appear to serve largely local demand. In several of the most important service sectors

Table 6.3 *Structure of employment,** 1986 (per cent of total employment)*

	Northern Ireland	United Kingdom
Agriculture	8.2	2.6
Mining	0.0	0.9
Manufacturing	18.5	22.3
Construction	5.7	6.1
Public utilities	1.6	1.3
Transport, communication	3.4	6.0
Private services	27.5	40.2
Government services	35.2	20.6

Sources: Dept of Employment, GB; Dept of Economic Development, NI.

ᵃ Including self-employment.

virtually all of the major firms are externally owned and this reduces the scope for selling services outside the region as the owning companies have their own branches in other parts of the UK and beyond.

The Northern Ireland private sector does not generate enough income from outside to support a population of 1.5 million people at current living standards, and the gap is filled by the public sector. Over 35 per cent of employees work directly for the government and another 7 per cent work for public corporations and other public sector organizations. In addition, public funds provide the main means of support for the one sixth of the labour force without jobs and partial support for others both in and out of the labour force.

As in all areas of high unemployment or low income, locally generated government revenue is not sufficient to finance a high level of public expenditure. Uniquely within the UK it is easy to identify the extent to which public expenditure in Northern Ireland is financed from outside the region. The current annual level of public expenditure is £5 billion. Locally-raised public revenues are equivalent to approximately two-thirds of this, and the final third is derived from an Exchequer grant or 'subvention'. This subvention may constitute as much as one third to one half of the total external income of Northern Ireland.[3] Although at first sight this would appear to be a major subsidy to a single part of the United

Kingdom it must be set within a context of the large range of national subsidies whose geographical incidence are unknown. Tax relief to home owners for example is likely to advantage the South-East of England more than other regions, as are transport subsidies. Moreover the redistribution of income through the tax and benefit system provides gains for all areas in which unemployment is high and incomes are low.

The large dependence on the public sector points up the weakness of the private sector. The latter is small relative to population and is itself dependent to a significant degree on demand generated by the public sector either directly through government expenditure or indirectly via the consumer spending of government employees. Future expansion of government spending is unlikely to be large, and the burden of growth must now be shouldered by the small private sector.

The role of economic research
The logic of the current economic situation thus leads towards an emphasis on improved competitiveness within the private sector. Three reports on Northern Ireland completed in the last three years all reflect this logic. The first of these is the Medium-Term Plan of the Northern Ireland Industrial Development Board, 1985. This emphasizes the development of profitable, expanding, companies and the encouragement of exports. The more traditional role of encouraging inward investment is now listed only third in the list of three priorities. Means of realizing the first two objectives include the encouragement of better marketing, new product development and use of up-to-date technology.

The second report, *Industrial Regeneration*, from the Confederation of British Industry's Northern Ireland Council, similarly emphasizes the regeneration of existing industry over inward investment (CBI, 1987). The report consists of 62 suggestions for promoting industrial regeneration, under six headings of which two are described here. Under the heading 'promoting business growth' the report emphasizes improvement of marketing, exporting and product quality. Suggestions on developing business education, vocation and skill, training and management education are made in the section on 'developing human resources'.

The latest of the three recent reports emphasizing improved competitiveness is the 'Pathfinder Report' of the Department of Economic Development (DED, 1987). This report represents current government thinking on the Northern Ireland economy and is produced by the Department responsible for most economic policy in the province including that of the Industrial Development

Board and its small firm equivalent the Local Enterprise Development Board. Pathfinder is particularly emphatic on the dangers of over-dependence on external sources for funding, ideas and initiatives. It aims to begin a process leading towards a stronger and less dependent economy. A starting point is to build on strengths. These, it would be generally agreed, include the advantage of small and close-knit economic networks, a pleasant physical environment, an industrial tradition with a reputation for quality, a mature education system and finally responsive and supportive public sector institutions. Despite these strengths problems remain. Six weaknesses are identified:

(1) lack of an enterprising tradition;
(2) deficiencies in training, work and managerial competence;
(3) distance penalties and small local markets;
(4) small manufacturing sector, large public sector;
(5) over-dependence on public funds;
(6) the political 'Troubles'.

A strategy for rectifying these weaknesses is outlined under the headings 'enterprise', 'competitiveness', 'exports', 'public sector' and 'use of public funds'. One part of the strategy involves engendering more positive attitudes to enterprise plus greater self-confidence among business starters. Another involves the concept of total Quality Management Audits to identify weaknesses in competitiveness. Other policy suggestions include 'internationalizing' management to improve exporting, and exporting services from the public sector.

Each of the reports is based on a wealth of direct experience of the operating conditions of business within the Province. It is probably fair to say however that none of the reports has been based on systematic economic research. Although a number of recent academic and consultancy studies have been undertaken on aspects of economic competitiveness no one would claim that these constitute a comprehensive or adequate understanding of the precise problem, or of the best avenues for progress. It is clear that further research is needed to aid the process of accelerating economic growth and that this must focus on the issue of competitiveness.

This research should involve pinpointing those areas of economic activity most capable of improvement. In part this may involve statistical comparisons, to reveal particular aspects of comparative inefficiency. However the availability of statistical information is already limited, and becomes more limited the closer one gets to issues involving commercial secrecy. To reach the heart of the issue of competitiveness economic research thus needs to employ a range of survey, interview and case-study work, although it is my belief that these methods are most effective in combination with statistical analysis.

Economic theory provides only rather general insights into questions of competitiveness especially within the context of a unified monetary union, which is of course the context within which Northern Ireland operates. Without a strong theoretical framework, or direct experience in commercial activity the most effective research strategy is likely to be that of comparative analysis. Operational practices within Northern Ireland companies and organizations can be compared with the best standards employed either within the local economy or in other areas. Such comparisons are inherently difficult due to the difficulty of focusing on the key variables, 'seeing the wood for the trees'. Good examples of the genre are all too rare, although one might single the work of Professor Prais and his colleagues at the National Institute for Economic and Social Research as a model, i.e. Prais (forthcoming), Daly, Hitchens and Wagner (1985), and Steedman and Wagner (1987).

Such research will involve experimentation and new methods. One possibility may be to combine the insights of academic economists with those of industrialists or consultants with commercial experience. Northern Ireland is likely to be a particularly favourable location for both undertaking and applying pathbreaking research of this type. It is a small region, hardly larger than the average English county. In the words of the Department of Economic Development's 'Pathfinder Report' it has 'the advantage of small and close-knit economic networks ... permitting swift transmission of knowledge and ideas and an effective pulling together to achieve better results.' In addition there is a widespread appreciation of the scale of economic problems and of the need for major economic improvement. This includes an acceptance of the need for research and a generally cooperative attitude towards providing data and other information. The well-established and close involvement of government with both industry and agriculture mean that once again the flow of information from the private sector is rather better than in other regions.

At the Northern Ireland Economic Research Centre the strategy for investigating competitiveness has begun with a number of 'ground-clearing exercises' to assess the best ways forward in undertaking research on competitiveness. One of these concerns the question of labour productivity. Even a brief examination of the official statistics on industrial production reveals the fact that output per employee in Northern Ireland manufacturing is well below the national average. The figure varies from year to year but is on average 15–20 per cent below the national level.[4] Not all sectors have low productivity, and a number of firms and industries have excellent records in this respect. However in other sectors the gap is large. Preliminary research suggests that differences in mix of industry and size of plant are insufficient to account for a gap of this magnitude.

Low output per employee as measured by the Census of Production may indicate either a problem of physical productivity, i.e. a low number of units produced per person or alternatively a problem of value added. In the latter case the number of units produced per person may be adequate but the value of the units may be deficient due to poor quality, design or marketing. Research is thus underway to attempt to separate these two broad possibilities. It will then be possible to build upon the results of this work to penetrate further into the complex questions of production, design and marketing. Since many firms in Northern Ireland have excellent records in these respects, an efficient research strategy will involve a concentration on those sectors which are lagging in comparison to the highest standards both within and outside Northern Ireland. One significant possibility is that major differences in competitiveness exist between locally-owned companies and those branch plants established by multinational and multi-regional companies. Research is currently being conducted to examine productivity differences between these sectors.

Low labour productivity will usually be associated with low wages and an aim of economic development policy should be to achieve high wages and thus high productivity. While it may be true that companies can realize acceptable return on capital if low productivity is matched by low wages, such operations within developed countries are vulnerable both to competition from less developed countries, and to wage pressures emanating from more affluent regions. In Northern Ireland the evidence suggests that while wages are below the UK average, labour productivity is even further below average, suggesting that labour costs per unit of output are high. If this is the case, then without offsetting cost advantages in other respects, either prices must be high or profits low. In the former case market share will suffer and firms will grow slowly or decline. In the latter case return on capital will be inadequate unless government grants are large enough to compensate. This last possibility puts a question-mark over the role of such grants. Further work is needed to indicate whether the grants themselves may be implicated in the continuing low level of productivity.

There is a widespread belief within Northern Ireland that an improved industrial performance depends on better management. While this is likely to be true almost by definition, the role of economic research should be to articulate and define those aspects of management most in need of improvement. The points above contain some suggestions, but a wide range of research is needed. One important facet is that of labour relations and wage bargaining. Existing work on strikes (Black, 1987) and wages (Harris and Wass, 1987) is helping to fill significant gaps in understanding.

A second ground-clearing exercise involves an examination not of surviving firms as in the above case, but of firms which have withdrawn from the province. Even if surviving firms were found to be efficient and profitable it may be the case that some classes of industry find Northern Ireland an uncongenial location. To investigate, and perhaps eliminate, this possibility research at NIERC is investigating the 70 branch-plant closures which have occurred since 1980, taking with them almost a quarter of Northern Ireland's industrial employment. One of the large questions in regional economic development must now be whether a strategy of inward investment can ever provide a stable long-term basis for growth. Although many nations have developed successfully on this basis due to raw material endowments or expanding domestic markets, it is less obvious that regions can do the same when the main attractions are labour availability and capital grants. Research on closures should help to shed light on the vulnerability of branch plants especially under conditions of widespread over capacity in recession.

A third project is on new and small firms. A very long-term view of economic development highlights the importance of small and new firms. Many of the largest indigenous companies in the UK were founded as small businesses in the early years of this century or in the inter-war period. Large numbers of well-established family firms have also been established since the last war, and much of the growth of the very largest companies has occurred through acquisition of thriving young businesses as they emerge into the medium-size categories.

Regions capable of producing large numbers of competitive new businesses are at a major advantage. Areas with a vibrant entrepreneurial base have in the past often generated jobs faster than the local labour market can expand, and thus 'export' economic activity. Other areas must rely on inward investment from these job-exporting regions. Increasing evidence suggests that the South of England has a distinct advantage in this respect. One comparison comparing Leicestershire with Cleveland showed how in the former county large numbers of jobs had been generated in the postwar period by new manufacturing firms without the help of government grants. In Cleveland few jobs were generated in this way and large-scale government assistance was needed to attract firms to fill the gap (Fothergill and Gudgin, 1982). The question of the formation of new companies and the growth of both new and other small firms is a complex one, requiring much research. Innovative comparative work by Hitchens and O'Farrell has suggested a problem of slow growth in small firms in Northern Ireland and has made major strides in explaining slow growth in terms of quality and price of production (Hitchens and O'Farrell, 1986). Initial work at NIERC has concentrated on establishing the facts on formation rates, growth and closure of small companies. This involves detailed comparisons with other parts of the UK and Ireland. Once the comparative facts are established survey work will be conducted to explain the differences.

Conclusion

Building on the results of these projects and other research already undertaken on the Northern Ireland economy, it is intended to evolve a research strategy which will develop ideas for increasing competitiveness and growth. Future projects will tackle aspects of managerial competence and will spread beyond manufacturing, into the service sector for instance. Much needs to be done and the likelihood of success will be enhanced if cooperation can be achieved between researchers in a number of universities and research centres. The types of research envisaged extend beyond the traditional concerns of academic economics and into research areas which are usually the preserve of business schools or even development agencies. The ultimate boundaries are far from clear but what is certain is that the economics' profession in a country like the UK and *a fortiori* in a region like Northern Ireland can no longer justify the degree of academic aloofness which has often characterized it in the past.

Notes

1. This calculation makes allowance for the fact that not all working-age migrants join the labour force and that unemployed people receive income in the form of benefits which increases demand for local services and hence creates jobs. Finally an increase in the labour force through lower migration inflates the denominator of the unemployment rate calculation as well as the numerator.

2. The *ex ante* change in the labour force is the change which would have occurred in the absence of out-migration. It includes actual change in labour force plus out-migrants of working age. An estimate of how many of the migrants would have participated in the labour force is obtained by applying the base-year ratio of labour force to working-age population.

3. External income as defined here as earnings from exports of goods and services, property income from outside Northern Ireland, and the government subvention.

4. Gross value added per employee calculated from the Census of Production.

References

Black, B. (1987) 'Collaboration or conflict: Strike activity in Northern Ireland'; *Industrial Relations Journal,* vol. 18 no. 1.

Confederation of British Industry (1987) *Industrial Regeneration: Action for Northern Ireland,* Belfast: CBI.

Department of Economic Development (1987) *Building a Stronger Economy: The Pathfinder Process,* Belfast: DED.

Daly, A., Hitchens, D.M.W.N. and Wagner, K. (1985) *Productivity, machinery and skills in a sample of British and German manufacturing plants,* NIER no. 111, London: NIER.

Fothergill, S. and Gudgin, G. (1982) *Unequal Growth: Employment Change in Cities and Regions,* Heinemann. London.

Harris, R. and Wass, V.J. (1987) 'The effect of collective bargaining on earnings in Northern Ireland in 1973', *Econ. & Social Review,* Vol. 19 No. 1.

Hitchens, D. and O'Farrell, P. (1987) 'The comparative performance of small manufacturing companies in Northern Ireland and South-East England', *Regional Studies,* Vol. 21, No. 6.

Prais, S. (forthcoming) *Training of British and German Foreman,* London: NIER.

Steedman, A. and Wagner, K. (1987) *A Second Look at Productivity Machinery and Skills in Britain and Germany* NIER No. 122, London: NIER.

7 Employment change in indigenously and externally-owned manufacturing activity in Northern Ireland, 1970–1980
Paul J. Bull

This chapter is concerned with employment change in indigenously and externally-owned manufacturing activity in Northern Ireland during the decade of the 1970s. The chapter begins with a justification for this approach. The empirical data used for this study have been obtained from a hitherto unused source, namely the Northern Ireland Industrial Training Executive, and the characteristics of this information source are described in some detail in the following text. An analysis is then undertaken, by industrial sector, of aggregate employment trends in the two ownership groups identified.

Location of ownership and control
There are two sets of reasons why a knowledge of the location of ownership and control of economic activity may be important for an understanding of the economic development of a region such as Northern Ireland. The first concerns the degree to which economic activity is owned and controlled externally, that is from outside the region under study. The possible advantages, and in particular the disadvantages, of external ownership for a regional economy have generated a substantial literature (Firn, 1975; Townroe, 1975; Hood and Young, 1976; Smith, 1979; Dicken 1980; Law, 1980; Watts, 1981). Although a region will, of course, benefit from the growth of externally-owned activity within its boundaries by the creation of jobs and the positive multiplier effects resulting from the payment of wages and the purchasing of local services and material inputs, its future growth and prosperity may also be impeded or truncated by their behaviour. The most important reasons for such effects would include:

(1) The movement of strategic decision-making from the region to corporate headquarters where they will relate to the corporation as a whole. Thus, the continuance and scale of an individual branch plant or affiliate may not depend on its

individual competitiveness or profitability, but on how it fits into wider corporate investment and development strategies.

(2) The opening of regional economies increasingly to the vagaries of international economic trends and to the internationalization of capital. Consequently, branches in regions with a relatively low rate of profit may be closed or reduced in size in favour of more profitable investments elsewhere. Thus, in times of national, or even international, recession externally-owned plants may shed labour and close branches more rapidly than locally-owned activity, not simply for reasons of corporate retrenchment, but also for the investment of scarce resources in the most profitable locations worldwide.

(3) Lower than expected local multiplier effects, due to in-house sourcing within large corporations.

(4) The loss from the region of high-calibre management. Local management may be attracted to externally-owned firms by relatively high real wages. Such individuals may then be lost from the region as they achieve promotion within the corporation.

(5) In problem regional economies externally-owned firms may be able to outbid indigenous activity for the limited industrial development (ID) assistance available from government sources. There are two reasons for this. First, by virtue of their careful monitoring of the external environment they may be more aware of available ID support for a particular region than even its indigenous sector, and second because of the larger size of project externally-owned firms may be able to offer.

During the post-1945 period a large number of externally-owned firms were encouraged, with the aid of generous ID grants, to establish manufacturing branch plants in Northern Ireland. As a result, a large proportion of the province's manufacturing activity is owned by firms headquarters outside the region. Indeed, Harrison (1982) has shown that in 1979 81.8 per cent of ID-assisted employment was controlled by externally-owned firms, which accounted for at least 37 per cent of the total manufacturing workforce at that time. However, as yet there is no knowledge of the non-ID-assisted external sector, and as a result no estimate of the proportion of all manufacturing employment in the province controlled externally, or locally. This chapter will provide such an estimate for the major manufacturing industries in Northern Ireland during the 1970s.

No attempt has so far been made to carry out a full assessment of the impact of externally-owned activity in Northern Ireland. On the positive side externally-owned business, with the aid of substantial

ID financial assistance, has provided a large number of jobs in the manufacturing sector since 1945: over 1.1 million job years by 1982 (Harrison, 1986a). On the negative side, two points can be made. First, Hoare (1978) has reported only a minor degree of interlinkage between the external sector and the local economy. The second point relates to the stability of externally-owned employment during periods of recession. Before the first major recession of the 1970s no firm conclusion on this issue had been reached for any of the British regions. However, recent evidence for some of the regions of Northern Britain (Henderson, 1979; Lloyd and Shutt, 1985), including ID-assisted activity in Northern Ireland (Harrison, 1986a), has demonstrated that externally-owned employment during periods of recession in the 1970s was more unstable in aggregate than indigenous employment. However, this has not yet been investigated for all manufacturing in the province. This chapter will begin such an analysis for the 1970s. The other possible problems associated with a high degree of regional economic dependence on the externally-owned and controlled sector have not been investigated in Northern Ireland.

The second reason for the need for information on the location of ownership of manufacturing activity in Northern Ireland is more pragmatic. Since the beginning of the 1970s, it has proved extremely difficult to attract externally-owned activity to the province. Reasons for this include the general reduction in mobile investment locating in the problem regions of the UK as a consequence of severe and persistent periods of recession, and the political instability of the province which may have diverted potential investment elsewhere (Bull and Hart, 1987). As a result, the province has had increasingly to look to the expansion of existing business (both indigenously and externally-owned) and to new indigenous activity for the maintenance and generation of new employment opportunities. While such a shift of emphasis appears to have been accepted rather reluctantly by the principal development agencies in the province, it has led to an enhanced and successful role for the Local Enterprise Development Unit (LEDU), established in 1972, whose remit has been to promote small manufacturing - and more recently service - businesses with less than 50 employees. In fact, between 1975 and 1985, the number of jobs promoted by LEDU increased from approximately 800 to 4000 per year (Northern Ireland Economic Council, 1986). Unfortunately (as will be noted in the next section) with the exception of work on ID-assisted industry, very little light has been shed on the characteristics of indigenous manufacturing activity by previous research. For example, the types of local businesses most resilient to employment loss since 1970 are not known. Yet in an era when external capital appears to show a marked disinterest in Northern Ireland, which cannot be explained simply by recession (Simpson, 1984), the importance of the indigenous sector for the future prosperity of the province cannot be over emphasised. As a result, an analysis of employment trends in indigenously-owned manufacturing activity will form one of the principal emphases of this chapter.

Indigenously-owned manufacturing activity

Until recently the quality of indigenousness rarely formed a direct focus for research on Northern Ireland manufacturing activity although, of course, there has been some outstanding work undertaken on important industries such as the linen complex (Steed, 1971, 1974) in which local ownership predominated. For the post-1970 era four areas of research providing evidence on the locally-owned sector are worth considering: industry studies, linkages, government-assisted industry and small firms. Chapter 12 is concerned exclusively with the small firm topic and therefore it will not be discussed here at any length. However, it is worth noting that despite serious doubts over this sector's competitiveness (Hitchins and O'Farrell, 1985, 1986) small plants with less than 50 employees were the only size-band of establishments in the province to record an absolute increase of employment between 1971 and 1981. Unfortunately, the increase was only 0.9 per cent compared with an overall decline in manufacturing of 31.8 per cent (Bull and Hart, 1987). Over the last ten years there has been a number of excellent studies of individual industrial sectors in the province, principally in a series of industry strategy documents by the Northern Ireland Economic Council (NIEC)[1], but also of the shipbuilding industry by Harrison (1986b). In some cases, such as the NIEC (1984) report on engineering, valuable insights into local business have been provided. Unfortunately, in general, no deductions about the indigenous sector can be made from these sector studies because most industries in the province are dominated by large externally-owned firms and few of the reports devote any space specifically to local businesses.

One of the most important findings of linkage research in Northern Ireland has been the local orientation of indigenous manufacturing activity. A result which applied as much to the small firm sector in Belfast in 1979 (Hart, 1985) as to local engineering and metalworking firms in the mid-1970s (Hoare, 1978). This latter result was in complete contrast to the other firms in these industries whose supplies, markets and managerial outlook were externally-oriented. Clearly, if such an inward-looking attitude continues to exist among indigenous businesses in Northern Ireland it will form a substantial constraint on their future growth prospects.

Research on ID-assisted industry has tended to indicate the relative success of locally-owned business activity in contrast to the externally-owned sector. For example, over the period 1945–79 indigenously-owned ID-assisted projects recorded a closure rate of 33 per cent compared to the much higher rate of 43 per cent for all ID-assisted projects. (Bull et al., 1982). Furthermore, Harrison (1986a) has demonstrated that throughout the 1970s indigenously-owned ID projects provided more stable employment opportunities in aggregate than the externally-owned sector. For example, between 1974 and 1979 the Northern Ireland ownership group lost ID-assisted employment at a rate of only −0.3 per cent compared with −4.6 per cent for externally-owned industry. However, for three reasons these findings do not necessarily indicate either the job-generating capacity or the long-term stability of the indigenous ID sector. First, indigenous ID projects have tended to be much smaller than other ID projects. In September 1979, for example, the average employment of an assisted project of Northern Ireland origin was 73 in contrast to 237 for GB and 460 for US projects (Bull et al. 1982). Thus far more of them will be required to generate a given number of jobs. Second, since most indigenous ID-assisted projects were set up in the 1970s, in stark contrast to the externally-owned group whose principal period of in-migration was during the 1960s, enough time has not yet elapsed to demonstrate their relative longevity or stability. As a consequence of these first two points it should also be noted that indigenous business has accounted for the far fewer ID-assisted jobs than the external sector since 1945. In fact between 1945 and 1982 Northern Ireland firms generated only 20.3 per cent of the total 1,427,000 ID-assisted job years (NIEC, 1983). Third, during the 1970s and early 1980s indigenous industry made far more use of job maintenance schemes – that is financial support to keep people employed – than other nationality groups. Indeed, in terms of the total number of projects receiving such support between 1971 and 1983 the Northern Ireland ownership group accounted for 52.6 per cent. And of the 286,022 job years of maintained employment the indigenous group accounted for 35.8 per cent (NIEC, 1985a). Thus a proportion of this indigenous job stability is more apparent than real. It does not stem from the profitability and efficiency of local firms which have received ID support but from additional government aid to prevent them from making redundancies.

Table 7.1   *ITE employment as a proportion of total employees in employment by industry group, 1970-80*

Date	Food and drink	Engineering A	B	Textiles	Clothing and fur
1970	94.9	74.8	85.2	93.9	98.8
1971	92.4	76.5	88.6	100.4	97.9
1972	92.9	80.4	94.0	98.1	96.0
1973	92.5	72.9	85.5	96.8	100.6
1974	90.8	71.5	84.4	93.7	95.6
1975	98.2	70.4	84.0	92.7	95.6
1976	90.9	67.5	82.4	94.2	98.3
1977	95.8	65.9	81.7	94.0	99.1
1978	91.9	64.4	78.8	*	102.4
1979	88.5	66.2	80.1	*	96.8
1980	88.2	64.1	76.3	*	93.3

A: Orders 7 to 12 inclusive of the 1968 SIC

B: Excluding orders 8 and 10.

* Sectoral employment excluding man-made fibres was not available for these years.

Sources: The Northern Ireland *Abstract of Statistics* and the DMS *Gazette for Northern Ireland.*

Data sources

The principal source of employment data for this investigation was obtained from the Northern Ireland Industrial Training Executive (ITE). The executive provided annual paypoint information for the period 1970-80 for all the enterprises they had contacted in four training boards:

(1)   Food and drink, defined by order 3 of the 1968 Standard Industrial Classification (SIC).
(2)   Engineering, orders 7-12 inclusive of the 1968 SIC.
(3)   Textiles, order 13 of the 1968 SIC, excluding man-made fibres (minimum list heading 411).
(4)   Clothing and footwear, orders 14 and 15 of the 1968 SIC.

In total, employment information for 1423 valid paypoints was obtained. Total employment covered varied from 124,329 in 1970 to 77,513 in 1980 representing 70 and 60 per cent respectively of total manufacturing employment in the province. For this project the data were restructured in four important ways.

(1) *Alteration to engineering*

From Table 7.1 it can be seen that the ITE data encompassed the vast majority of employment in each of the four individual training boards. In the food and drink, textiles, and clothing sectors coverage was never lower than 88 per cent of official estimates derived from the annual census of employment. Admittedly, given first that the ITE employment estimates refer to April and the official estimates to June, and second that employment in general was in decline, an inflated estimate of employment coverage is to be expected. Nevertheless, the consistently high level of employment coverage over the whole ten years strongly indicates that the ITE data is representative of real employment trends. The employment coverage in engineering was initially disappointingly low and over time somewhat erratic. Lower results were perhaps to be expected in such a broadly-defined training board in a sector which is typified by many small-sized, and therefore perhaps difficult-to-enumerate, units. (NIEC, 1984). However, on inspection of the individual SIC orders within engineering under-representation was found to be principally the result of a very poor employment coverage in instrument engineering and shipbuilding and marine engineering. The removal of these two orders increased the percentage employment coverage to that shown in Table 7.1.

(2) *Amalgamation of paypoints*

Paypoints are theoretically an unsatisfactory unit of analysis because above the level of the single-plant firm they need not refer exclusively to either the firm (the decision-making and legal unit) or the establishment (the smallest production unit). For example, a firm with five plants in a particular area may have any number of paypoints from one to five, and as a result paypoints cannot be used directly for any detailed analysis of locational change. Furthermore, the firm may change this number through time without the number of establishments changing at all. Such a reorganization of paypoints was taking place in some firms in Northern Ireland during the 1970s, giving the impression of establishment closure where no such event had occurred. As a consequence for this analysis, paypoints have been amalgamated into 'firm' or enterprise units. Thus the observations refer to consistent units for analysis namely the total activities of individual firms within Northern Ireland.

Table 7.2 Ratio of ITE to CL employment

Year	All cases	Food and drink	Engineering	Textiles	Clothing and fur
1970	102.5	121.2	103.9	94.1	103.2
1971	97.2	116.8	94.3	100.5	100.2
1972	105.2	108.7	108.8	101.9	98.0
1973	101.0	85.9	102.5	98.9	102.7
1974	102.9	93.8	106.6	96.9	100.4
1975	105.2	115.0	108.5	95.7	101.9
1976	90.4	104.2	82.2	104.9	104.6
1977	102.4	108.3	99.0	106.6	106.8
1978	102.0	95.0	102.6	102.0	102.9
1979	100.9	104.8	102.5	92.9	103.4
1980	100.5	112.4	100.6	92.9	102.3

(3) *Exclusion of small firms*
From the beginning of the study period, 1970, three of the four training boards enforced minimum size criteria for inclusion in their activities. The exception was clothing, but this board included a minimum size of 25 employees the following year. The minimum sizes at that time in the other boards were textiles five employees, engineering an annual wage bill of £7500 and food and drink an annual wage bill of £15,000. These criteria, which since 1976 have all been in financial terms, have been revised upwards a number of times during the 1970s. Therefore the small firm sector is both poorly and inconsistently represented by the ITE information. This may well account for some of the under-representation of employment in the engineering board. As a result it was decided to delete all firms with fewer than 50 employees from the analysis. This is unfortunate, because the 1970s in Northern Ireland represents a decade in which small establishments became relatively more important in employment terms (Hart, 1986). Nevertheless, for reasons of internal consistencey such a decision was necessary.

(4) *Cabinet List corroboration*
Annual employment data on all government assisted projects (excluding the small firms assisted by LEDU) are officially recorded on the Cabinet List (CL). This in-house record, used in the calculation and monitoring of financial assistance to firms, should in theory be one of the most reliable employment data sets in the

province. A comparison of the employment records of firms existing in both ITE and CL sources can be found in Table 7.2. The very high degree of concurrence in all sectors adds support to the contention that the ITE data provide a consistently accurate set of data for the analysis of employment change in a large proportion of the manufacturing sector of Northern Ireland during the 1970s.

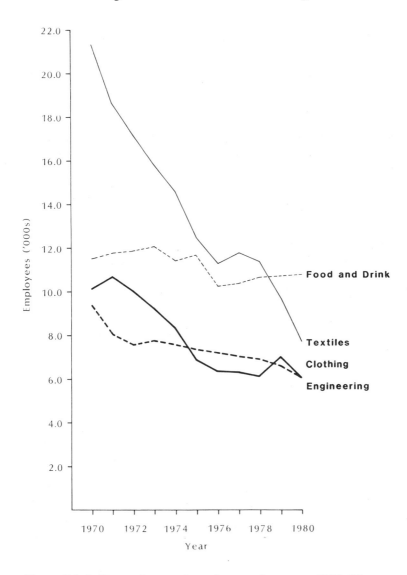

Figure 7.1 Indigenously-owned employment by sector, 1970–80

For each enterprise in the ITE file the location of ownership was obtained using either standard directories such as *Who Owns Whom* and *UK Kompass* or from the Northern Ireland Companies Registry in Belfast. Changes in ownership during the period were also noted. Thus location of ownership in this investigation is in terms of the location of ultimate ownership as defined by Firn (1975) and has been divided into two classes: indigenous or local (within Northern Ireland) ownership, and external (outside Northern Ireland) ownership. Unfortunately, in this analysis it has not been possible to take account of the varying degrees of local control which exists in the externally-owned enterprises in the province.

Employment change in indigenously and externally-owned activity

The trends in indigenously-owned employment in enterprises with 50 or more employees in the four ITE industrial sectors described above can be seen in Figure 7.1. The general feature is one of decline ranging from the massive employment loss in textiles of over 13,000 jobs, or 63 per cent, to the rather modest decline by Northern Ireland standards of only 7.6 per cent (less than 1000 jobs) in food and drink. In between, substantial employment reductions of 40.7 per cent and 35.6 per cent took place in clothing and engineering respectively. As a result, with the exception of food and drink, the 1970s in Northern Ireland witnessed very large reductions indeed of indigenously-owned employment in the most important manufacturing industries in the province (Harrison, 1982 Bull and Hart, 1987).

Figure 7.1 also shows that employment decline was not constant over the decade of the 1970s and gives the distinct impression that employment loss in clothing and engineering was less in the second half of the period. This is borne out by the evidence in Table 7.3 which details rates of employment change in the two five-year periods: 1970–75 and 1975–80. This table also demonstrates that indigenous employment loss in textiles was also less in the latter half of the decade. However, in both engineering and textiles the differences in the rates of decline either side of 1975 are very small. The food and drink industry displays markedly different trends. In the first half of the period an actual employment gain was recorded of 1.4 per cent. However, the 8.9 per cent loss in 1975–80, much of which, according to the NIEC (1985b) strategy report on the industry, was the result of contraction in the meat processing industry following increased feed costs after joining the EEC, generated an overall employment decline during the decade of 7.6 per cent.

Table 7.3 *Employment change in indigenously-owned manufacturing activity, 1970-75 and 1975-80 by industrial sector*

| | Percentage employment change | | |
	1970-75	1975-80	1970-80
Food and drink	1.4	- 8.9	- 7.6
Engineering	-20.4	-19.1	-35.6
Textiles	-41.8	-37.2	-63.6
Clothing	-33.1	-11.4	-40.7

Table 7.4 *Employment change in externally-owned manufacturing activity, 1970-75 and 1975-80 by industrial sector*

| | Percentage employment change | | |
	1970-75	1975-80	1970-80
Food and drink	- 3.8	-12.5	-15.8
Engineering	- 4.0	-18.2	-21.5
Textiles	- 8.1	-37.8	-42.8
Clothing	-22.9	- 4.1	-26.0

Except for the food and drink industry therefore the indigenously-owned businesses in the other three major Northern Ireland manufacturing industries lost jobs at an alarming rate during the 1970s. But how did these rates of decline compare with the external sector? Was the Northern Ireland sector more resilient than the externally-owned one to employment loss during this time? A comparison of Tables 7.3 and 7.4 shows that for the period as a whole rates of externally-owned employment decline were much lower in engineering, textiles and clothing and higher in food and drink. Thus in this last industry Northern Ireland businesses were in aggregate providing more stable employment opportunities than their externally-owned counterparts. However, if this comparison includes the two five-year periods 1970-75 and 1975-80, major differences can be observed both within the externally-owned group (Table 7.4) and between the two ownership groups (Tables 7.3 and 7.4). Apart from in the clothing industry, externally-owned employment loss was much larger in the second half of the decade than in the first, with the largest deline of all of 37.8 per cent taking place in textiles. Northern Ireland therefore would appear to have been becoming an increasingly unattractive location for externally-owned investment in these industries as the decade of the 1970s progressed. Furthermore, during the latter half of the decade the rates of employment change in the external group were much closer to the indigenous rates than during the first half of the period. Indeed, in food and drink and marginally in textiles the rate of employment loss after 1975 was smallest in the indigenous group. Thus between 1975 and 1980 aggregate employment stability was greater in the indigenous sector in these two industries than in the external one. A finding which reinforces in a general sense for two industries in the province the result noted earlier for ID-assisted firms only.

The relative success of the indigenous sector in the latter half of the 1970s can also be seen in Figure 7.2. Here indigenously-owned employment is depicted as a percentage of total employment by industry. As a result the percentage share of indigenously-owned employment will rise when rates of employment loss over any annual period are less for the indigenous than for the externally-owned sector. The favourable performances of food and drink, textiles and engineering between 1975 and 1978 can clearly be seen.

Figure 7.2 also shows the relative importance of indigenous employment by industry during the 1970s. Thus, in the food and drink industry and even in textiles, despite substantial relative losses between 1970 and 1976, more than 50 per cent of employment was owned locally. However, it is the relatively small share of employment in engineering that is of particular importance. At no time during the 1970s did the local sector own more than 29 per cent of employment in enterprises with 50 or more employees in engineering. Furthermore, at least 55 per cent of this employment was accounted for by one company – Mackies, the textile engineering firm.[2] In 1984 the NIEC strategy document for engineering stated that 'a good engineering infrastructure is vital for the development of an advanced economy. It is essential for manufacturing efficiency which in turn is an important determinant of competitiveness' (NIEC, 1984: 1). Unfortunately, an industry heavily dominated by externally-owned firms, which if similar to those existing in the mid-1970s in the province have few local linkage contracts, may not be able to provide such an infrastructure and as a result may seriously jeopardize the province's future growth prospects.

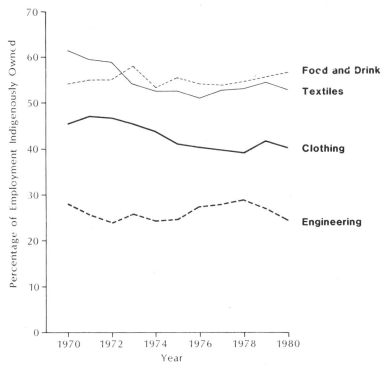

Fugure 7.2 Percentage of employment indigenously owned by sector, 1970-80

Net entrant and *in situ* employment change

The employment changes described above are the result of the actions of individual firms to open or close their enterprises, or to expand or contract existing workforces (*in situ* change). In addition, merger and takeover activity may result in a firm moving from one ownership group to another.[3] The ITE data file permits a detailed analysis of all these components of regional employment change. In this chapter space permits just a few brief remarks on two: employment generated by new firms, and *in situ* employment change in businesses which continued to trade throughout the 1970s.

Table 7.5 shows that the indigenous sector rather than externally-owned firms recorded the highest rates net job creation[4] between 1970 and 1980. Only in textiles did externally-owned activity account for more net new jobs in 1980 than the indigenously-owned group. Of course, these results give no indication of the gross number of new jobs provided by these two ownership groups during the 1970s, but they do point once more to the rather better performance of the local sector towards the end of the decade. However, because these rates of new entrant employment for both ownership groups are small the vast majority of jobs in all four industrial sectors in 1980 were offered by firms which had remained in existence throughout the study period. Indeed, the actual employment proportions provided by all surviving enterprises in food and drink, engineering, textiles and clothing were 88.5, 91.4, 87.4 and 89.8 per cent respectively. Unfortunately, comparative work on other problem regions of the United Kingdom for the same time-period and industrial categorization is not available. Nevertheless research findings in regions as diverse as Merseyside between 1966 and 1975 (Lloyd, 1975) and the Coventry region 1974–82 (Healey and Clark, 1984) tend to indicate that these proportions are far from exceptional. In addition, in regions such as Northern Ireland where job-creation through local business formation and branch-plant in-migration has proved difficult since the end of the 1960s for a series of economic, political and social reasons, they emphasize the important of nurturing existing enterprise. However, despite a range of ID policies since the early 1970s to encourage firms both to re-equip and to counter redundancy plans, aggregate employment stability in enterprises which survived the study period has been extremely variable.

Table 7.5 Net entrant employment rates,* 1970–80, by ownership group and industrial sector

| | Net entrant employment rates, 1970–80 (%) | |
	Indigenously-owned	Externally-owned
Food and drink	7.3	2.9
Engineering	3.5	2.9
Textiles	1.8	3.8
Clothing	3.8	3.0

* Employment in firms new to the ITE register 1971–80 inclusive, which were still in existence in 1980, as a proportion of total employment in 1970.

NB Ownership change between the two ownership groups is not regarded in this analysis as a generator of new employment.

In Table 7.6 *in situ* employment change for the 1970s is recorded by ownership group and industrial sector. The greatest variation in rates of employment change occurred between industries in the indigenous ownership group. Here employment actually increased in the food and drink industry by 8.6 per cent and declined only slightly (−1.5 per cent) in clothing, whereas in engineering and textiles substantial rates of employment loss in excess of 35 per cent took place. Nevertheless the rates of decline in textiles, and especially in clothing, were much lower than for total employment decline in these industries, and along with the positive result in the food and drink industry indicate that in three major industrial groups in the province enterprises which had remained in existence throughout the 1970s had a greater ability to provide both stable aggregate employment opportunities and net employment increases than the net result of enterprise openings and closures. To a lesser degree this result is also true for externally-owned activity in engineering, textiles and clothing. The relative success of surviving firms may well be the result of ID employment maintenance schemes. Unfortunately, such a conclusion cannot be reached from the scale of analysis undertaken here.

Table 7.6 In situ employment change, 1970–80, by ownership group and industrial sector

| | In situ employment change 1970–80 (%) | |
	Indigenously-owned	Externally-owned
Food and drink	+ 8.6	−18.7
Engineering	−37.1	− 9.2
Textiles	−42.5	−37.0
Clothing	− 1.5	−16.9

NB In these calculations ownership change between the indigenously and externally-owned sectors was not taken into account. That is ownership was defined soley in terms of the group to which an enterprise belonged in 1970. Only in textiles did any major ownership changes take place between these two groups during the 1970s. As a result a net shift of 892 jobs to the externally owned sector took place. Taking this into account the *in situ* employment rates of change would be −48.9 per cent for the indigenous group and -25.4 for the externally-owned group.

In addition, the evidence in Table 7.6 also demonstrates that, with the exception of textiles, substantial differences in *in situ* employment change can be found between the ownership groups. The results in clothing and food and drink are particularly noteworthy because they indicate a much more favourable employment performance in indigenously-owned enterprises which survived the decade than in externally-owned ones.

Conclusion

This chapter has presented for the first time virtually comprehensive location-of-ownership information for enterprises with 50 or more employees in the four most important manufacturing industry groups in Northern Ireland during the 1970s. The degree of external ownership varied between the industrial sectors. In textiles and food and drink it accounted for less than 50 per cent of total employment throughout the study period. Whereas in engineering externally-owned enterprises encompassed over 70 per cent of total employment. It was suggested that this may prove to be a serious weakness in the engineering infrastructure of the province.

During the 1970s major employment losses took place in all the industries under study except in the food and drink industry, and since both ownership groups took part in this decline no major changes in the proportion of employment externally-owned took place. Nevertheless over the decade as a whole employment loss in indigenously-owned enterprises was larger than in the externally-owned sector in all industries except once again in food and drink. However, there were signs that during the latter half of the decade the rate of employment loss in externally-owned enterprises had increased, which would, of course, tend to replicate wider employment trends in multi-locational enterprises in western capitalist economies following the first major recession of the mid-1970s. Indeed, as a consequence during the latter half of the 1970s, the rate of employment loss was larger in the externally-owned sector than in indigenously-owned enterprises in both the food and drink and the clothing industries. Finally, information was presented on the very low rate of net entrant employment creation during the study period. This pointed to the importance in terms of job provision in Northern Ireland of enterprises which had remained in existence throughout the 1970s.

Notes
1. At the time of writing the NIEC have published industry strategy reports on textiles; engineering; distribution; food, drink and tobacco; wood and paper; rubber, chemicals and plastics; non-metallic mineral products; and clothing.

2. The most important externally-owned employer in engineering in Northern Ireland was Short Brothers, the armaments and aircraft manufacturers, wholly owned by the UK government since the late 1960s. Its employment ranged from 22 per cent in 1972 to 35 per cent in 1980 of total externally-owned employment in this sector.

3. The only major ownership changes between the externally and indigenously-owned groups took place in textiles. By 1980 the indigenous sector suffered a net loss of 892 jobs to the externally-owned group.

4. New firms to the ITE file include:
   1. Entirely new enterprises with 50 or more employees.
   2. Existing enterprises expanding their workforce to 50 or more employees.

References

Bull, P.J., Harrison, R.T. and Hart, M. (1982) 'Government assisted manufacturing activity in a peripheral region of the United Kingdom: Northern Ireland 1945–1979'. In Collins, L. (ed). *Industrial Decline and Regeneration*, Dept of Geography and Centre for Canadian Studies, University of Edinburgh.

Bull, P.J. and Hart, M. (1987) 'Northern Ireland', In Damesick, P.J. and Wood P.A. (eds). *Regional Problems, Problem Regions and Public Policy in the United Kingdom*, Oxford: Oxford University Press.

Dicken, P. (1980) 'Foreign direct investment in European manufacturing industry: the changing position of the United Kingdom as a host country'. *Geoforum* 11: 289–313.

Firn, J.R. (1975) 'External control and regional development'. *Environment and Planning A* 7: 393–414.

Lloyd, P.E. and Shutt, J. (1985) 'Recession and restructuring in the North-West region, 1974–82: the implications of recent events'. In Massey D. and Meegan R. (eds). *Politics and Method: contrasting studies in industrial geography*, London: Methuen.

Harrison, R.T. (1982) 'Assisted industry, employment stability and industrial decline: some evidence from Northern Ireland'. *Regional Studies* 16: 267–85.

Harrison, R.T. (1986a) 'Industrial development policy and the restructuring of the Northern Ireland economy'. *Environment and Planning C* 4: 53–70.

Harrison, R.T. (1986b) 'Inter-organisational relations, technical change and industrial geography: studies in the development of the UK shipbuilding industry'. Unpublished PhD theses, Queen's University, Belfast.

Hart, M. (1985) 'The small firm: an evaluation of its role in the manufacturing sector of the Belfast urban area'. Unpublished PhD thesis, Queen's University, Belfast.

Hayter, R. (1982) 'Truncation, the international firm and regional policy'. *Area* 14: 277–82.

Healey, M and Clark, D. (1984) 'Industrial change in Coventry: 1974–1982'. *Local economy research papers* 5, Dept of Geography, Lanchester Polytechnic, Coventry.

Henderson, R.A. (1979) 'An analysis of closures amongst Scottish manufacturing plants'. *Economics and Statistics Unit Discussion Papers* 3. Scottish Planning Dept, Edinburgh.

Hitchins, D.M.W.N. and O'Farrell, P.N. (1985) 'Inter-regional comparisons of small firm performance'. Dept of Economics Occasional Paper 24, Queen's University, Belfast.

Hitchins, D.M.W.N. and O'Farrell, P.N. (1986) 'The comparative performance of small manufacturing companies in South Wales and Northern Ireland: an analysis of matched pairs'. Dept of Economics Occasional Paper 25, Queen's University, Belfast.

Hoare, A.G. (1978) 'Industrial linkages and the dual economy: the case of Northern Ireland'. *Regional Studies* 12: 167–180.

Hood, N. and Young, S. (1976) 'US investment in Scotland - aspects of the branch factory syndrome'. *Scottish Journal of Political Economy* 23: 276-94.

Law, C.M. (1980) 'The foreign company: location investment decision and its role in British regional development'. *Tijdsch. Econ. Soc. Geogr.* 71: 15-20.

Lloyd, P.E. (1979) 'The components of industrial change for Merseyside Inner Area: 1966-1975'. *Urban Studies* 16: 45-60.

NIEC (1983) 'The duration of Industrial Development Assisted Employment'. *Report 40.* Northern Ireland Economic Development Office, Belfast.

NIEC (1984) 'Economy strategy: the Engineering Industry'. *Report 46.* Northern Ireland Economic Development Office, Belfast.

NIEC (1985a) 'The duration of Industrial Development Maintained Employment'. *Report 52.* Northern Ireland Economic Development Office, Belfast.

NIEC (1985b) 'Economic strategy: food, drink and tobacco'. *Report 51.* Northern Ireland Economic Development Office, Belfast.

NIEC (1986) 'Economic strategy: Industrial Development'. *Report 60.* Northern Ireland Economic Development Office, Belfast.

Simpson, J.V. (1984) 'An investigation into the employment generated by new industry locating in Northern Ireland, 1951-80'. Unpublished paper read to the Statistical and Social Enquiry Society of Ireland, Dept of Economics, Queen's University, Belfast.

Smith, I.J. (1979) 'The effects of external takeovers on manufacturing employment change in the Northern region between 1963 and 1973'. *Regional Studies* 13: 421-38.

Steed, G.F.P. (1971) 'Industrial organisation, firm integration and locational change: the Northern Ireland linen complex 1954-1964'. *Economic Geography* 47: 371-83.

Steed, G.F.P. (1974) 'The Northern Ireland linen complex 1960-1970'. *Annals of the Association of American Geographers* 64, 397-408.

Townroe, P.M. (1975) 'Branch plants and regional development'. *Tn. Plann. Rev.* 46: 47-62.

Watts, H.D. (1981) *The branch Plant Economy: a study of external control* London: Longman.

8 Small manufacturing firms in Belfast and Glasgow: the implications of backwards and forwards linkages
Alan Middleton

One of three fundamental characteristics of small firms identified by the Bolton Report was that they should be independent, in the sense that they do not form part of a larger enterprise, and that the owner-managers should be free from outside control in taking their principal decisions (Bolton Report, 1971: 1-2). These formally independent firms are distinguished from small subsidiaries which may have a high degree of independence but whose ultimate authority lies elsewhere. It is independence which also distinguishes the small business from the franchised operation, although there is evidence that there is a difference between formal control and operational control in franchised businesses. This makes the difference in independence between the conventional small firm and the franchised operation one of degree rather than an absolute. (Stanworth et al., 1984: 174).

Bolton recognized that effective control of small business may be circumscribed by obligation to financial institutions, but it is also clear that effective decision-making is conditioned by the insertion of a firm in its wider economic context. The market imposes itself on independence, and networks of economic interaction impose limits on the logical choices available to small businessmen. Not only is the small firm owner dependent on the state of the economy for the general well-being of his firm (CBI, 1979), but his insertion in that economy and the direct linkages which he has with other actors in it limit his independence and condition his firm's development. Small companies grow and decline in response to environmental threats and opportunities (Gibb and Dyson 1984, 251). For these firms, with their strong orientation to their local economies, differences in the immediate environment can have a substantial impact on the choices which are available to the small firm owner. The differences between locations with respect to sources of supply and market outlets can therefore be extremely important for small firm development potential – much more than may be the case for larger firms. It is also our contention, however, that this environment is structured and has an underlying logic which must be understood by policy-makers.

There is not only the competition between enterprises, which neo-classical economics stresses as the determinant of industrial structure, but there are also backward and forward linkages between enterprises which determine flows of value and the pattern of accumulation. These linkages also have a spatial dimension and the geographical location of enterprises and consumers at different points on the chain of production and distribution can have important implications for the development of a local economy. It is often stated, for example, that industry and employment in Scotland and Northern Ireland would suffer greatly if the manufacturers of these regions were cut off from the rest of the UK market. This matter is very much related to thorny constitutional questions in the minds of many people and, since it is embedded in the political rhetoric of both regions, it is of considerable ideological importance. It is, however, also an empirical question which ought to be investigated more fully. What is the pattern of accumulation within which industries are located, and how does this affect local economies? What is the nature of the linkages between firms within the process of accumulation? These questions take us beyond the gross trade flow statistics which show, for example, that there is a greater volume of trade between Northern Ireland and Great Britain than there is between North and South. They lead us to look more closely at the position of small firms and how they relate to the wider economy.

There are two distinct perspectives on the relationships between small and large companies. On the one hand, there are those who see such relationships as benign. In this case it is assumed that linkages with large-scale firms are good for small firms, supplying the latter with inputs and markets which permit them to accumulate and grow in size. Large firms are also assumed to benefit, since interactions create new opportunities for these large-scale companies: as the large firms grow, their activities become more complex and it becomes economic to spin off some new specialized work to small subcontractors and suppliers (Bannock, 1981: 100).

This image of a high-tech relationship between small and large is contradicted by the second perspective which emphasizes exploitation in small-large interactions. This exploitation is seen to be operating on two levels. First, it is considered to be a feature of inter-firm relations, such that encouragement of competition between small firms forces down the prices of the inputs of large-scale capital. Secondly, the exploitative relationship also invades the internal relations and working conditions of the small firm. It has been argued that there are many instances of small firms doing big business's bidding, being totally controlled by and dependent on a number of bigger firms. For example, the output of many small sweatshops goes to big retail firms and the continued expansion of the backstreet clothing industry is contrasted with the collapse of large-scale production in this sector (Davis and Green, 1979: 46). Large companies gain the advantage of low-wage production, giving them more competitive prices in the mass market – without the odium of directly employing people in extremely poor working conditions. They exercise control over many small suppliers and can force down prices by threatening changes in purchasing policy which would close the small factories and render their workforces redundant (ibid, 47). It has been argued that the future of small businesses in the US is, in fact, one in which they would only exist in clusters of small cottage industries which would act as feeders to the industrial giants, supplying them with equipment, parts and support services (*Business Week*, September 1979, quoted by Thompson and Leyden, 1983: 39).

This chapter looks at the forward and backward linkages of small independent companies in Belfast and Glasgow in order to throw some light on the nature of the relationships which exist. This will lead us to develop a number of policy issues for small firms in Northern Ireland. First, we shall deal with backward linkages and the various sources of inputs into the small manufacturing firm. We shall look at the differences between the two cities with respect to these linkages and try to assess some of the implications of these differences for the development of small firms and the local economy. We shall then go on to consider forward linkages to the consumers of the products of the small firms and to identify those linkages which could be crucial for policies aimed at the growth of small firm employment.[1]

The structure of supply

Constraints on the supply of inputs

Historically, the physical isolation of Northern Ireland from the rest of the United Kingdom means that it is cut off from supplies of essential raw materials and capital inputs. In the latter half of the nineteenth century, the development of the province was hindered by the non-availability of the raw materials of the industrial revolution – coal and iron (Green, 1976: 92; Goldstrom, 1976: 111). The engineering and shipbuilding sectors of Belfast grew despite this weakness in the economy, but the fact that these materials and the products of their combination had to be transported across the Irish Sea has had implications for both the cost of production and the structure of production and distribution in the province.

At the present time, we are interested in the extent to which the fact that small producers in Belfast are more likely than those in Glasgow to be cut off from a direct source of supply of raw materials and capital goods restricts their access to these inputs. Transport cost will be higher, but we would also like to know if there is an additional factor of monopoly supply which could affect the Northern Ireland entrepreneur disproportionately. Monopoly supply restricts the choices available to the entrepreneur and therefore impinges on his independence and his freedom within the market, it may further increase his input costs, and it could be a factor in restricting his access to new technology. The question which arises is whether the Belfast firms have a limited number of suppliers.

The overall picture is one of a diversity of supply in both cities (Table 8.1). Nevertheless, the small firms in Belfast do suffer greater constraints on their freedom to choose, and therefore on their independence, since they are twice as likely as those in Glasgow to have only one source of raw materials. A slightly lower percentage in both cities report a single supply of machinery and the difference between the cities in this case is not significant. That is, the Belfast firms apparently suffer no comparative disadvantage with respect to access to capital goods and new technology through monopoly supply. The restrictions on the supply of raw materials are indeed likely to be translated into higher prices, but the Belfast firms should not have to pay more for capital goods and new technology. this, however, leads us to the question of the structure of supply. Are the Belfast firms at a disadvantage in that they do not have direct access to the producers of inputs and have to rely disproportionately on wholesalers whose prices will be higher?

Table 8.1 Companies with a single source of supply for raw materials and machinery

	Both cities		Glasgow		Belfast		Significance
	No.	%	No.	%	No.	%	
Raw materials							
Only 1 source	71	13	26	9	45	18	
More than 1 source	460	87	254	91	206	82	0.0052
Machinery							
Only 1 source	43	8	18	7	25	10	
More than 1 source	481	92	259	93	222	90	0.1773

Types of supplier
The types of firm which supply the inputs are reasonably varied
and the most common source of supply of raw materials in both
cities is through wholesalers (Table 8.2). It would appear that the
geographical separation of Belfast does not lead the small producers
in this city to rely on one or other source more than the small
manufacturers in Glasgow. Neither are they more inclined to
purchase directly from manufacturers of raw materials on the
mainland because of the lack of outlets in Belfast; nor do they have
to make more use of wholesalers in the absence of local producers.
The only significant difference between the two cities with respect
to source of supply of raw materials is that the Belfast producers
are much more likely to use retailers than their counterparts in
Glasgow. The numbers however are small.

When buying machinery the pattern of supply is different. In
both cities the majority of firms purchase their machinery directly
from the producers or their representatives. Wholesalers are the
second most important category of supplier but the Belfast firms are
more likely to mention this source than those in Glasgow. As might
be expected, retailers are not important suppliers of machinery but
a sizeable proportion of firms mentioned 'other' sources of supply.

*Table 8.2 From whom inputs were purchased
(% of firms mentioning each source)*

	Both cities No.	%	Glasgow No.	%	Belfast No.	%	Significance
Raw materials							
Producers or their representatives	280	52	140	50	140	55	0.2789
Wholesalers or their representatives	321	60	172	61	149	58	0.5628
Retailers	20	4	4	1	16	6	0.0063
Others	23	4	14	5	9	4	0.5377
Machinery							
Producers or their representatives	292	54	157	56	135	53	0.5187
Wholesalers or their representatives	175	33	80	28	95	37	0.0417
Retailers	20	4	8	3	12	5	0.3703
Others	119	22	71	25	48	19	0.0867

These were mainly sources of second-hand machinery, such as the auctions which occur when other companies are forced to close down. The overall picture of these backward linkages therefore is one in which wholesalers or their representatives are the major suppliers of raw materials or their representatives are the major suppliers of raw materials while direct purchase from producers is the main means of acquiring machinery. Nevertheless, the small manufacturers in Belfast are more reliant on wholesalers for their capital inputs than those in Glasgow.

The potential impact on employment
The use of wholesalers for the purchase of inputs means that in the majority of cases, the part of the investment which goes towards the purchase of inputs passes directly to large-scale merchants and then on to large-scale producers. Clearly, the structure and the geography of supply can be important for local multiplier effects. If the suppliers are locally based there may be a further impact on local investment and employment through the further investment of profits deriving from small manufacturing investment. However, wholesale operations create few local employment opportunities and are unlikely to lead to the creation of local jobs in small-scale manufacturing firms. Whether or not they create local employment in large-scale firms will depend on the location of their suppliers. If the manufacturers of the inputs are local firms, the purchase of these goods by small firms can lead to profit and further investment in the locality. If they are not local producers, the profit which accrues is likely to be invested elsewhere. The questions which now arise are where the producers of the inputs are located and whether the situation in Belfast is different from that in Glasgow.

The spatial distribution of supply and demand

The location of suppliers
From the evidence we have gathered we cannot provide information about the original sources of materials and capital coming through wholesalers. Small producers are unlikely to be able to give accurate information on the location of ultimate producers of inputs bought through intermediaries. Nor did we ask any questions which would permit us to identify locally-based or externally-based wholesalers. We felt that we could not expect small producers to be able to give us this information either. Where the small firm owner did deal directly with the producers of his inputs we asked for further information on the location of the supplying company and their size.

The striking feature of our results is the heavy dependence of both Glasgow and Belfast firms on manufacturers from other parts of the UK and to a lesser extent from the countries of the Common Market (Table 8.3). Almost three-quarters of small firms in the sample as a whole purchase raw materials from other parts of the UK outside Scotland and Northern Ireland and two-thirds get their machinery from the same geographical source. What is also surprising is that, despite the larger industrial base of West Central Scotland, the firms in Glasgow were just as likely as those in Belfast to get raw materials and machinery from the rest of the UK. We retested to find out if the Glasgow firms were more likely than the Belfast firms to get raw materials from their immediate environment and discovered that 49 per cent of the Glasgow firms bought raw materials in Scotland and 43 per cent of the Belfast companies bought them in Ireland, both North and South.

We expected to find a certain amount of interchange of goods between Scotland and Ireland, but the amount of trade was small and was all one-way. A handful of firms in Belfast bought raw materials and machinery from Scotland but not one small firm in Glasgow bought any of its inputs from Northern Ireland. The common feature of small firms in both Glasgow and Belfast was their heavy reliance on distant producers. They provide a market for external manufacturers, particularly from England and, perhaps, Wales.

This raises serious questions about local employment strategies based on encouraging capital investment in small firms. The evidence here suggests that finance for the purchase of locally-produced raw materials would have a greater impact on local employment than finance for capital inputs. To go even further, finance for capital inputs in labour saving machinery is likely to replace local jobs and channel public funds back to England or overseas. The argument proposed by government and its small firm agencies, that public finance to small firms should set off a cycle of wealth-creation leading to investment and then to the creation of employment may be undermined by these findings. The cycle of local wealth-creation is broken and the imported new technology is labour-replacing. It would appear that the structure of supply will ensure that investment-oriented policies (rather than policies which directly concern themselves with the creation of employment) may lead to further employment decline and a continuing weakening of local markets. The evidence also suggests that financial assistance for the purchase of locally-produced raw materials would have a greater impact on local employment than finance for capital inputs.

Table 8.3 Geographical source of inputs[a]

| | Both cities | | Glasgow | | Belfast | | Significance |
	No.	%	No.	%	No.	%	
Raw materials							
Belfast area	34	12	0	0	34	24	—
Other part of NI	32	11	0	0	32	23	—
Republic of Ireland	15	5	0	0	15	11	—
Glasgow area	41	15	38	27	3	2	—
Other part of Strathclyde	25	9	24	17	1	1	—
Other part of Scotland	38	14	34	24	4	3	—
Other part of UK	204	73	103	74	101	72	0.8931
EC	62	22	26	19	36	26	0.1952
Other	47	17	27	19	20	14	0.3374
Machinery							
Belfast area	11	4	0	0	11	8	—
Other part of NI	5	2	0	0	5	4	—
Republic of Ireland	4	1	0	0	4	3	—
Glasgow area	17	6	16	10	1	1	—
Other part of Strathclyde	1	—	1	1	0	0	—
Other part of Scotland	8	3	7	5	1	1	—
Other part of UK	193	66	101	64	92	69	0.5133
EC	99	34	56	36	43	32	0.6043
Other	80	27	49	31	31	23	0.1488

[a] For those companies who obtained inputs from producers or their representatives. Other firms were excluded on the assumption that they were unlikely to know the origin of the materials if they did not deal with the producers.

A further issue concerns the size of the firms which supply the inputs. The producers of inputs are mainly large-scale firms (Table 8.4). Only a minority of small manufacturers purchase their inputs directly from other small-scale producers. There was no difference between the cities on the size distribution of the companies with which the small firms had backward linkages. The implication of this is that not only does investment by small firms contribute to a geographical concentration of wealth outside their local economies, but it also leads to a concentration of accumulation in large firms.

Table 8.4 *Size of companies which produce and supply inputs*

Size	Raw materials[a]		Machinery[b]	
	No.	%	No.	%
L.T. 7	22	8	8	3
7–25	33	12	8	3
26–100	42	15	17	6
101–200	42	15	39	13
M.T. 200	172	61	202	69
Don't know	37	13	43	15

[a] Data refer to the 280 small companies who obtained raw materials from producers or their representatives.

[b] Data refer to the 292 small companies who obtained machinery from producers or their representatives. In this case, Belfast firms were more likely to mention size range 101–200 than Glasgow companies.

Public policy which subsidizes capital investment in small firms may therefore be leading to employment displacement in these enterprises and accumulation in large firms in other parts of the UK. This could be acceptable if such investment increased the ability of the small firms in Glasgow and Belfast to compete in the wider UK or European market: increased competitiveness raises the possibility of enterprise survival and at least some job retention. However, this argument only holds if small firms are in fact in competition with firms in the wider economy. To the extent that they are unable to penetrate wider markets and are in competition with each other within a *local* stagnant or declining economy, increased competitiveness based on capital investment can mean fewer firms with less employment surviving at the expense of others. This raises the question as to where the markets for small firms in Glasgow and Belfast are, and with whom they are in competition.

The location of customers
As we have suggested, it has almost become a truism that the economy of Northern Ireland is highly dependent on its relationship with Great Britain. In the nineteenth century, successful large-scale Irish industry was export-oriented, while those firms which depended to a large extent on the domestic market declined. It was only by developing export markets that manufacturing firms could

reach a scale of production which would enable them to survive in the home market against foreign competition (Cullen, 1972: 157). Incoming investment in the twentieth century was also export-oriented. Since the Second World War, for example, projects of investment from Great Britain represent one third of the total number of projects assisted in the province and 54 per cent the total job-years created (NIEC, 1983: 24). Although many of these projects, mainly dating from the 1940s and 1950s, have now closed, they were oriented towards the British market.

In contrast, the firms in our survey were very much oriented towards their immediate locality. When we asked where they were selling their products around 95 per cent indicated that they sold in the city in which they were located (Table 8.5). The Belfast firms were more oriented towards the regional economy than the Glasgow firms and, significantly, 48 per cent of the Belfast firms had customers in the Republic of Ireland.

Table 8.5 Where the small manufacturers sell their products [a]

	Both cities		Glasgow		Belfast		Significance
	No.	%	No.	%	No.	%	
Belfast area	253	47	7	3	246	96	0.0000
Other part of NI	240	45	6	2	234	91	0.0000
Republic of Ireland	130	24	7	3	123	48	0.0000
Glasgow area	285	53	269	95	16	6	0.0000
Other part of Strathclyde	229	43	211	75	18	7	0.0000
Other part of Scotland	196	36	172	61	24	9	0.0000
Other part of UK	194	36	112	40	82	32	0.0724
EC	47	9	28	10	19	7	0.3737
Other	58	11	24	9	34	13	0.1038
Total number of firms	539		282		257		

[a] % refers to the percentage of firms mentioning a particular market.

There was very little interrelationship between Northern Ireland and Scotland, although there was a greater likelihood that the Belfast firms would sell in Scotland. Few of the Glasgow firms had customers in Northern Ireland. On the other hand, there was no difference between the cities in the orientation of the small firms to the rest of the market outside Scotland and Ireland. The Belfast firms were slightly less likely to sell in England and Wales than the

Scottish firms but the difference is not statistically significant. The existence of markets in the EEC and elsewhere was limited and the differences between the cities were not significant. Only around 10 per cent of the small manufacturers sold products in these markets.

The number of Belfast firms selling in the Republic of Ireland was greater than those selling in England and Wales and while just over one third sell products in Great Britain (i.e. including Scotland), almost half of the small firms in Belfast sell in the Republic of Ireland. Great Britain is clearly more important as a supplier of imports than as a market for production (Table 8.6). The Northern Ireland companies exist as a market for British production, while their own markets are highly localized and they are more likely to sell in the Republic of Ireland than Great Britain.

There are a number of implications which flow from this. First, it is relevant for the constitutional issue in Northern Ireland and, secondly, it raises more general economic policy issues. The constitutional issue is obviously the most delicate, but it has to be confronted by those who are concerned with economic policy in Northern Ireland. If policy for the economic regeneration of the province is to have an important small firm component, it has to be recognized that the South is already a more important market for small firms than the rest of the UK and that this market may offer some capacity for expansion. The institutional mechanisms for this already exist through the Anglo-Irish Agreement. To move further in this direction, however, would fly in the face of the wishes of the majority community in Northern Ireland. Some members of that community have in fact threatened to disrupt the trade which already exists between North and South in order to protect their constitutional position. Such disruption could have serious consequences for small firms in Belfast from both sides of the communal divide.

Table 8.6 Relationship of small firms in Belfast to suppliers and markets in the UK and the Republic of Ireland

	Total no. of relevant firms	Republic of Ireland no. of firms	% of firms	Great Britain no. of firms	% of firms
Source of raw materials[a]	140	15	11	104	74
Source of machinery[a]	134	4	3	93	69
Market for products[b]	257	123	48	89	35

[a] For those firms who get their inputs directly from the producers.
[b] Including the companies selling in Scotland.

Since we are not dealing here with information about the value of business between North and South it has to be said that the small firms may only be selling a small part of their production in the South. Some firms are unwilling to increase their level of business with the Southern companies because of the feeling that they may not be paid for their goods. On the other hand, it is difficult to get information on this since a number of firms also have bank accounts in the South which they would not like the UK taxman to know about. What is perhaps called for is an organization which can promote linkages between small firms on either side of the border and at the same time offer legal protection against the failure of customers to pay. At present, small companies cannot contemplate the legal costs involved in pursuing their intersts in a different legal system.

With respect to the more general economic policy issues, the findings suggest a number of conclusions which are relevant for the development of the local economy. First, that small firms policy in Northern Ireland which is based on assistance with capital investment leads to a flow of funds out of the province for the purchase of inputs. Consequently, there is little local multiplier effect, with most of the benefits being experienced in other parts of the UK. Secondly, labour-saving machinery increases the competitiveness of some small firms to the detriment of others in what is a highly localized market. The result is the displacement of labour and other small firms with no guarantee that the firm with the higher level of technology will even attempt to penetrate wider markets. Thirdly, the policy of providing assistance with capital investment for all sectors of small-scale manufacturing, irrespective of their potential for export earnings, ought to be reconsidered, with some thought being given to the possibility of investment incentives being related to the purchase of local inputs and/or export performance. Fourthly, given the narrowness of the markets North and South, 'local' should be defined as 'all-Ireland' and a means of coordinating small-scale activities in both areas ought to be pursued. Fifthly, before it is possible to develop alternative policies along these lines, more information is needed about the structure of demand for small firms and about what types of firms are most likely to benefit from new policies. In the next part of this chapter we shall try to throw some light on this by looking at the structure of demand for small firm production.

The structure of demand

The final consumers
The forward linkages of small-scale manufacturers to the rest of the economy provide small producers with access to the markets for their goods. The commodities produced by small-scale manufacturing may be consumed directly by the general public, may re-enter the process of production through their incorporation as raw materials or capital by the private sector or they may be purchased by the state, either to be consumed in the provision of services or in the production processes of nationalized industries. To reach these consumers, goods may be transferred directly or they may arrive via intermediaries. Levels of demand for different firms may vary according to the buoyancy or depression of the different segments to which they are oriented and may be restricted by a narrow structure of access to markets.

The small manufacturers are meeting demand from the general public, the private sector and the state. Taking both cities together, 80 per cent of small manufacturers produce goods for other firms in the private sector (Table 8.7).[2] These are goods which will re-enter the processes of production and distribution.[3] Fifty-eight per cent produce goods which are consumed by the general public and 57 per cent produce for the public sector. Despite, or perhaps because of, the acknowledged narrowness of the market in Northern Ireland, the Belfast firms had a wider range of types of customer than those based in Glasgow. They were much more likely to sell to the general public, the private sector and the public sector than the Glasgow firms.

Two-thirds of the Belfast firms produced goods which were used by the general public, while just over half of those in Glasgow did so. Similarly, the Belfast firms were more likely to produce for other private sector firms than were the Glasgow companies. What is most significant, however, is that 71 per cent of small manufacturers in Belfast produce goods for the public sector, compared to only 44 per cent in Glasgow. We shall return to this later, but it is clear that the fortunes of small firms in Belfast are more closely tied to the fate of the public sector than those in Glasgow.

Taking the two cities together, the most important private sector consumers are service sector firms. Half of the small firms produced goods which were consumed by service companies. The next largest group of consumers were in manufacturing, followed by construction. However, the relationships between small firms and these sectors of the economy were different in each of the cities.

Table 8.7 Customers of small manufacturers in Belfast and Glasgow

	Total %	Glasgow %	Belfast %	Significance
General public	58	53	64	0.0127
Private Sector	80	74	87	0.0002
Agriculture	14	10	19	0.0024
Manufacturing	46	46	46	0.9625
Construction	35	33	37	0.4283
Services	51	38	65	0.0000
Other	52	50	55	0.3009
Public sector	57	44	71	0.0000
The government or local authority	50	38	62	0.0000
Nationalized Industries	22	27	16	0.0038
Other	10	16	5	0.0000

The service sector is much more important for Belfast firms than for those in Glasgow. In fact, the greater likelihood of Belfast firms producing for the private sector is mainly due to the importance of the service sector as a customer in the city. This may be mainly a reflection of the structure of the Belfast local economy, but it is nevertheless significant that 65 per cent of the Belfast firms produced for service sector companies, compared to only 38 per cent in Glasgow.

This raises the question as to what the effect of capital assistance to firms in the service sector in Belfast might be for stimulating small-scale manufacturing, particular if this assistance is linked to a 'buy locally' policy. Stimulating service sector capital spending in Belfast will have greater impact on small firms than the same strategy in Glasgow.

In addition, the Belfast firms were much more likely than Glasgow companies to provide inputs for agriculture. Again, this is to some extent a reflection of the greater importance of the sector in the Northern Ireland economy, but it does raise the further question as to how agricultural policy can be linked to small firm development in the province.

There is no difference between the cities with respect to production for manufacturing and for the construction industry. However, while in Belfast it is the service sector which provides the most important private sector outlet for small-scale manufacturing production, in Glasgow manufacturing is dominant. Within the public sector, it is clear that the purchasing role of central government and council authorities can be extremely important. Taking the two cities together, half of the companies produce for government. The difference between Glasgow and Belfast, however, is highly significant. While 38 per cent of the companies in Glasgow produce goods which are purchased by the local or central state, in Belfast the figure is 62 per cent. This perhaps reflects the extent to which the state has penetrated the Northern Ireland economy and has become a dominant economic fact of the life for the province. However, it also raises further questions about the constitutional issue to which we shall return shortly.

The differences between the cities in the orientation of small firms to local and central government and their agencies contrasts with their relationship to the nationalized industries. A significantly higher proportion of small manufacturers in Glasgow produce for this type of customer than in Belfast.

In summary, when the small businesses in the two cities are combined and the consumers disaggregated, the largest identifiable group of producers are those oriented towards the general public. This is closely followed by those producing goods for service industries, the state and manufacturing. This composite picture, however, is made up of two distinct structures of demand in Glasgow and Belfast. In Glasgow, manufacturing is second in importance to the general public as a source of demand, with the state and the private service sector third equal. In Belfast, the private service sector, the general public and the state are almost equally important, each providing a market for over 60 per cent of the small manufacturers.

This suggests that raising demand from the general public would have the greatest overall impact on the fortunes of small firms in both cities. The fortunes of small firms are therefore indeed intimately linked to the fortunes of the economy as a whole. If a choice had to be made, however, between stimulating demand from either the manufacturing sector or services, the outcome would not be the same in each city. Small manufacturers in Glasgow would benefit more from a stimulation of manufacturing than firms in Belfast, while firms in this city would benefit from an increase in capital spending by the private service sector and the state. Once again we have to stress that a regional development policy which concentrates on assisting investment in manufacturing may not be the best possible alternative for local small-scale manufacturing as a whole.

Types of distributor
The small firm owners were asked how they distributed their goods to the consumers – whether they sold them directly or whether they passed through wholesalers, retailers or some other intermediaries. The extent to which the firms dealt directly with the final users of their products was related to who the consumers were. Taking the two cities together, between 75 per cent and 85 per cent of firms who sold to the different branches of activity in the private sector used direct sale only and around 90 per cent of sales to the public sector were done directly. In the distribution of small manufacturers' goods to the private and public sectors, therefore, very little additional employment is being created in commerce. In addition, 57 per cent of manufacturers whose products were destined for the general public had no other means of distribution other than their own sales outlets.

The method of supplying the general public was, however, significantly different in each city. Seventy-two per cent of the small firms in Belfast used their own outlets alone, compared to 40 per cent in Glasgow. The Glasgow firms had a far greater variety of outlets than the Belfast ones, reflecting a more complex market structure in the Scottish city. Once again, the evidence would suggest very little forward linkages which would be employment and income generating. This would further suggest that the benefits of any stimulation of demand for small manufacturers would be unlikely to be felt elsewhere in the local economy. Since there are few forward linkages through retail and wholesale outlets, there would be little stimulation of these sectors through increased small firm production.

Dependence on one main customer
The high level of direct contact between small firms and others in the economy brings us to the question of the extent to which small firms are dependent on the will or the fortunes of large firms. We have pointed to the two different perspectives on small firm/large firm relations: one viewing such relations as benign and assuming that any extension of linkages would be beneficial to both small and large firms, the other stressing the exploitative nature of these relationships whereby small firms are subordinated to the interests of large-scale capital. According to the latter perspective the relationships are not only economic, but also involve a power dynamic such that the small firm is at the mercy of the decision-making of larger one. This dependence and subordination increases to the extent that the small firms rely on one or a few large firms for the sale of their goods. The larger number of companies to which firms are selling and the more widely distributed is their

Table 8.8 *Percentage of production bought by main customers in Glasgow and Belfast*

	Both cities		Glasgow		Belfast	
	No.	%	No.	%	No.	%
Up to 10%	292	54	149	53	143	55
11–20%	83	15	52	18	31	12
21–30%	50	9	35	12	15	6
31–50%	39	7	23	8	16	6
More than 50%	75	14	23	8	52	20
Total	539	100	282	100	257	100

$x^2 = 24.80005$; 4 DF; Significance = 0.0001

production, the less will be their dependence on the will of any one firm. Once again, if we accept that there is a more restricted local market for the Belfast firms, we might expect small firms in the city to be dependent on a smaller number of companies than is the case in Glasgow.

There is, however, no differences between the cities with respect to the number of customers which the small firms have in the private sector and there is little evidence of the type of concentration of demand which would decrease the independence of small firms and subordinate them to the will of a few large companies. In order to gather further information on this, however, we also asked the firms how much of their production went to their principal customer.

Most of the small firms in both Glasgow and Belfast are not dependent on any single customer (Table 8.8). There was , however, a significant difference between the cities on this score. the firms in Belfast were more likely to be reliant on a single customer than those in Glasgow. One fifth of the small manufacturers in Belfast sold more than half of their production to a single outlet, compared to only 8 per cent of companies in Glasgow. These firms are extremely vulnerable to changes in the purchasing policies of other firms.

When asked what sizes of firms they produced for, 59 per cent said 'all sizes'. Nevertheless, there was a difference between the cities in that Belfast's small-scale production is more likely to be linked into other small-scale enterprises than Glasgow production (Table 8.9).

Table 8.9 *Size of private sector customers in Glasgow and Belfast*[a]

	Total	Glasgow No.	%	Befast No.	%
Firms with up to 25 employees	69	19	10	50	25
Firms with more than 25 employees	333	180	91	153	75
Total	402	199	100	203	100

$x^2 = 15.03518$; 1 DF; Significance = 0.0001

[a] Excluding those who did not have private sector customers and those who did not know the size of the firms they sold to.

Table 8.10 *Percentage of production bought by main customer, by size of small firm*

	Total no.	Size 1–10 no.	%	11–20 no.	%	21+ no.	%
Up to 10%	292	175	61	80	48	37	43
11–20%	83	39	14	32	19	12	14
21–30%	50	22	8	15	9	13	15
31–50%	39	18	6	13	8	8	9
More than 50%	75	33	12	26	16	16	19
Total	539	287	100	166	100	86	100

$x^2 = 15.73032$; 8 DF; Significance = 0.0464

Dependence on a single customer was also related to the size of the small firms, but not in the way that might be expected (Table 8.10). The *larger* the firm the greater its dependence on one large customer. Why this should be so is not clear but it may be that firms do grow on the basis of such contacts. On the other hand, this dependence does make them particularly vulnerable to changes in purchasing policy of the larger firms.

Implications for employment

Possibly the greatest impact on employment in small firms in both Glasgow and Belfast would derive from stimulating demand from the general public. That is, the future of small firms is intimately linked to the future of the economy in general and if the incomes and purchasing power of the people were to be raised this would reflect back on small-scale employment. Nevertheless, there are two other factors which are significant in Northern Ireland: the roles of the state and services as customers for small-scale production.

The most controversial is the role of the state, for, as we have suggested, this also impinges on the constitutional issue. We have already argued that more ought to be done to develop small firms' links between North and South, and this is likely to meet with opposition from one section of the community. In contrast, the implications of the scale of the relationship between small manufacturers and the state will cause concern to the other part of the community. Opposition to the existence of the British state in Northern Ireland also entails opposition to the employment which it generates, both directly and indirectly. Small manufacturing firms would benefit from an increase in public spending by the British government and any reduction in the activity of the public sector would be detrimental to many small firms and to employment within them. Any shift of the locus of the state to Dublin would have a similar effect and firms on both sides of the communal divide would be affected by any change.

Less controversial is the relationship between small producers and the service sector. Services provide the largest part of private sector customers. This implies that stimulation of the purchasing power of the service sector may have greater impact on small manufacturing employment than policies which encourage capital investment in manufacturing.

The linkages between small firms is greater in Belfast than in Glasgow and any policies which stimulate small manufacturing development in Northern Ireland are more likely to have a cumulative effect within this sector. However, a counterbalance to this is the fact that at present there are few forward linkages to retail and wholesale activities. Increasing the volume of demand for small-scale production would have little effect on employment and incomes in commerce. There would be little additional employment created outside small-scale manufacturing.

In addition, although the majority of companies in Belfast produce for a fairly large number of customers, a significant minority are dependent on single customers buying most of their production. This reduces the independence of these firms and makes them highly vulnerable. Attention should be paid to means of reducing this dependency and subordination in the longer-term interests of the small companies.

Conclusions
We have argued that effective decision-making and the choices open to small firm owners are conditioned by a firm's insertion in its wider economic context. The market imposes itself on apparent independence and networks of economic interaction create a limiting context for small firm growth. The direct linkages which the small firms have with other actors in the economy limit the small businessman's independence and condition his company's development. Since most small firms produce mainly for local markets, the local economic, social and political environment can have a substantial impact on the fate of these firms. It is therefore imperative that we understand the nature of local environments and how they impinge on the fortunes of small businesses.

Dependence on a single source of supply of inputs or reliance on one large customer places small firms in a precarious position, but few of the firms in our study were in this position. Linkages were characterized by a diversity of supply and of market outlets. Firms in Belfast, however, were more dependent than those in Glasgow. They were more likely to have only one source of supply of raw materials, and they were more likely to have one large customer for their output. In addition, they were more likely to use wholesalers for the purchase of their machinery, which is likely to mean higher costs with relatively few local jobs created through small firm purchasing.

One of the main characteristics of the small firms in both cities was their reliance on other parts of the UK for their inputs, with the implication of investment being channelled to large firms in other parts of the country as labour-saving machinery replaces local jobs. Since production is for a highly competitive local market, this calls into question the policy of non-discriminatory financial assistance for capital investment in small-scale manufacturing firms.

The most controversial findings relate to the constitutional question in Northern Ireland and have implications which will be resisted, for different reasons, by the different communities in the province. On the one hand, the number of Belfast firms selling to the Republic of Ireland is greater than those selling in the rest of the UK. Great Britain is more important as a supplier of inputs than as a market and if policy for regenerating the Northern Ireland economy is to be realistic it must take this into account. There would appear to be scope for the encouragement of these linkages, a policy which would be resisted by one part of the communal divide.

On the other hand, we also saw that the public sector in Northern Ireland is an important customer for small manufacturing firms. Reflecting the importance of the state in the economy of the province, almost two-thirds of the companies produce for the government. Increased government spending, which implies an increase in the role of the British state and which would be strongly opposed by another section of the community, would have a beneficial effect on small firm employment. Any decline in this expenditure or a shift of the locus of government to Dublin would be detrimental.

Policy-makers in Northern Ireland and the economists who provide them with analyses of the local economy would prefer to ignore these factors. They will, however, have to grasp this nettle, present the facts to both sides of the communal divide, and conduct a dialogue with political leaders on the implications for the economic development of the province.

The greatest influence on the well-being of small firms is the general state of the economy and the most potent stimulus would come from an increase in the living standards and purchasing power of the people of the province. Stimulation of small firms could be an element of this wider strategy. Since the service sector provides the largest share of the private sector market for small manufacturers, any stimultion of this sector would have an important impact on small manufacturing employment and would perhaps be more relevant than providing assistance for capital investment in an untargetted way.

The targeting of assistance would, however, require some knowledge of how different branches of production relate to their suppliers and their markets. Elsewhere in our research we have confirmed that the relationships between small manufacturers and the suppliers of inputs vary considerably for different branches of small firm production (Middleton and McEldowney, 1984: Chapter 8: Middleton, 1987: 21–6). First, whether they depend primarily on producers or wholesalers depends on both the type of economic activity of the small firms and the type of input being purchased.[4] Secondly, whether or not firms buy their raw material from other parts of the UK is also related to the branch of production in which the firms operate. Thirdly, the propensity to use British, EC or overseas suppliers of machinery varies according to the activity carried out by the small manufacturers. Fourthly, whether or not a company produces for the general public, the private sector or the public sector depends on the branch of production in which it is located. Fifthly, there is a strong relationship between the branch of small firm and the branch of its customers in the private sector.

An important question is whether public policy for the stimulation of local investment and employment can be designed to take these subtle variations in backwards and forwards linkages into account. At the present time we cannot elaborate on precisely how this might be done, but the facts suggest that there may be a case for the creation of micro-economic models which would allow more finely-tuned selective assistance policies to be pursued.

Acknowledgement

I would like to acknowledge the assistance of James J. McEldowney in the research reported in this chapter.

Notes

1. We interviewed a total of 539 small-scale manufacturing firms in the two cities; 282 were in Glasgow and 257 in Belfast. The companies interviewed were independent enterprises employing up to 25 persons within the Glasgow Inner Conurbation and the Belfast Urban Area. We applied a 23-page questionnaire which dealt with four main themes: the socio-economic situation of the entrepreneurs and their workforces, the internal and external structural relationships of small firms, the attitudes of entrepreneurs to different elements within these structures, and the orientation of the entrepreneurs to the future. The research therefore constituted one of the largest and most comprehensive surveys of small manufacturing firms conducted in the UK. In order to avoid embarrassing questions which could have been of interest to the taxman and which would have made the respondents more reluctant to participate, we did not ask about the financial operations of the firms. Such information is impossible to gather with any accuracy on this scale. It does mean, however, that we cannot say anything about the values of inputs and outputs.

2. When we asked the small manufacturers to identify the branch of activity in which his or her private sector customers were located he or she was not always able to do this. Consequently, the category of others contains a large number of firms.

3. The question which was asked referred to consumption, as distinct from articles which could be resold.

4. For example, whereas 68 per cent of food and drink manufacturers purchase their raw materials directly from producers, only 34 per cent of mechanical engineering firms use this direct source. Seventy-six per cent of the latter businesses deal with wholesalers compared to only 42 per cent of the former. The contact with producers or wholesalers also varies according to the type of input. For example, 40 per cent of printing and publishing firms buy their raw materials directly from producers, but 71 per cent buy their machinery directly. Seventy-eight per cent use wholesalers for raw materials but only 21 per cent purchase machinery through them. Only those companies in Timber and Wooden furniture consistently make more use of one type of source for all their inputs. They tend to buy their raw materials, and machinery through wholesalers.

References

Bannock, G. (1981) *The Economics of the Small Firm: Return from the Wilderness,* Oxford: Blackwell.

Dolton Report (1971) *Small Firms – Report of the Committee of Inquiry on Small Firms,* London: HMSO

Confederation of British Industry (1979) *Smaller Firms and the Inner City Problem,* London: CBI.

Cullen, L.M. (1972) *An Economic History of Ireland since 1660,* London: Batsford.

Cullen, L.M. (ed) (1976) *The Formation of the Irish Economy,* Cork: Mercier.

Davis, B. and Green, J. (1979) 'A Marxist view', in Loney and Allen (1979).

Gibb, A. and Dyson, J. (1984) Stimulating the growth of owner-managed firms, in Lewis et al. (1984) 249–75.

Goldstrom, J.M. (1976) 'The industrialisation of the North-East in Cullen, (ed.) (1976) 101–12.

Green, E.R.R. (1976) 'Industrial decline in the nineteenth century, in Cullen, L.M. (ed.) (1976) 89–100.

Lewis, J. et al. (1984) *Success and Failure in Small Businesses,* London: Gower.

Loney, M. and Allen, M. (1979) *The Crisis of the Inner City,* London: Macmillan.

Middleton, A. and McEldowney, J.J. (1984) *Structural and Cultural Constraints on Small-Scale Manufacturing Development in Glasgow and Belfast.* ESRC Report No. RDB 5/13/2.

Middleton, A. (1987) 'Small manufacturing firms in Glasgow and Belfast: the implications of backwards and forwards linkages. Paper presented to ESRC Conference on Economic and Social Research in Northern Ireland. Belfast: 7 January.

Northern Ireland Economic Council (1984) *The Duration of Industrial Development Assisted Employment.* Belfast: No. 40.

Stanworth, J. et al. (1982) *Perspectives on a Decade of Small Business Research.* Aldershot: Gower.

9 Relative earnings in Northern Ireland, 1972–1982
R.I.D. Harris

This chapter makes use of unpublished New Earnings Survey (NES) data to look at relative differences in average hourly earnings between Northern Ireland and the rest of the UK. Using this database, it is also possible to determine whether the differential is due to industrial structure (i.e. does Northern Ireland have more of its workforce employed in industries and/or occupations which are lower paying nationally?), or the different plant and company sizes operating in the province (given that there is a known positive relationship between size and earnings), or differences in institutional forces (i.e. collective bargaining structures). Using regional consumer price indices, it is also possible to consider to what extent relative earnings still diverge after allowing for differences in the regional cost of living. Lastly, it is important to note that the work reported here is of a preliminary nature, although the results presented do help to set an agenda for future research into the causes of differences in earnings between UK regions.

The differential between earnings in Northern Ireland and Great Britain

Figures 9.1a and 9.2a plot the relative position of Northern Ireland *vis-a-vis* the UK for males and females over the period 1972 to 1982. Information is also given for the GLC (which had the highest average hourly wage), the South-East, and East Anglia (the latter experiencing the lowest earnings for a region of GB). For males, relative earnings in the province were typically around 88 per cent of the UK average, 74 per cent of earnings in the GLC, and 96 per cent of earnings in East Anglia. There was some evidence that the gap between Northern Ireland and the latter region widened after 1977, although relative earnings drew closer together in 1982.

Turning to female relative earnings (Figure 9.2a), this shows that Northern Ireland tended to fluctuate around 88–90 per cent of the UK average, with clear evidence of a slight downward trend post-1976 (the exception being in 1980). The differential with the GLC was around 74 per cent, while Northern Ireland earnings for females were generally close to 94 per cent of those in East Anglia. Clearly, for both males and females, there was a persistent differential during the 1970s and early 1980s, despite a period during the 1960s when regional earnings differentials narrowed significantly (see Black, 1985).

We now turn to results in Figures 9.1b and 9.2b, which plot the relative position after allowing for differences in the cost of living in Northern Ireland *vis-a-vis* the rest of the UK.[1] Two general points emerge; first, the relative differences across regions are much narrower than before (note Figures 9.1a and 9.1b and 9.2a and 9.2b are drawn on the same scales). Secondly, the rankings of the regions have altered, primarily because of the higher costs of living in the

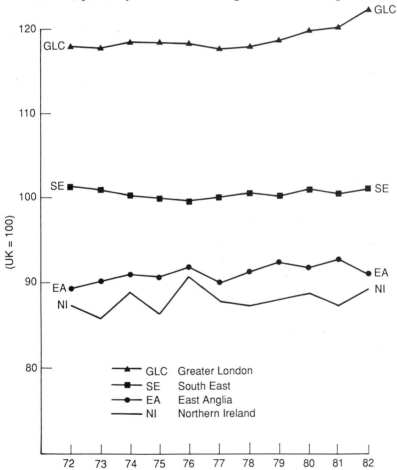

Figure 9.1a Relative hourly earnings males F/T, 1972–82

GLC and South-East regions (which is mostly to do with the relative costs of housing in these areas). Hence, regional differences at the aggregate level largely disappear when allowance is made for differences in the cost of living, and this needs to be borne in mind when analysing the size and importance of relative differentials at a more disaggregated level.

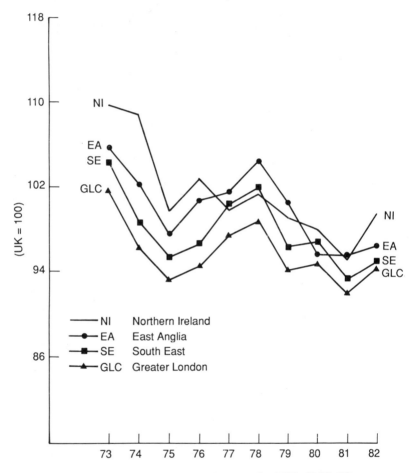

Figure 9.1b Real relative hourly earnings males F/T, 1972–82

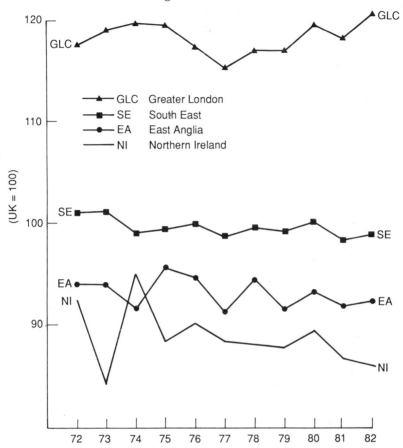

Figure 9.2a Relative hourly earnings females F/T, 1972-82

The earnings differential by industry and socio-economic group

Table 9.1 presents information on the size of the male differential in average hourly earnings, broken down by industry and SEG (Socio-Economic Group), for 1972 and 1982. It suggests that earnings in Northern Ireland are consistently low across different groups of workers (excepting manual workers in agriculture), and therefore that these differentials are due to characteristics associated with the regional economy as a whole (e.g. the lower cost of living demonstrated above). To confirm this, Figures 9.3 and 9.4 plot actual and 'expected' relative earnings for males and females, where the latter series is obtained after adjusting for differences in

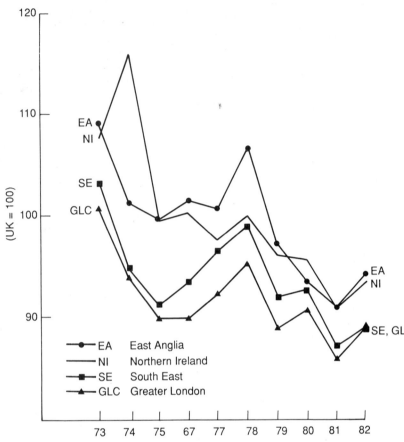

Figure 9.2b Real relative hourly earnings females F/T, 1972–82

industrial structure between the Province and the UK.[2] It can be
seen that dependence (in employment terms) upon low-paying
industries only 'explains' a small proportion of the regional
differential (typically less than one per cent for males and a much
smaller percentage for females).

A further test of the importance of earnings differentials is to
rank relative earnings for each SEG and industry division from
highest to lowest, calculate the mean rank for each region and
compare this to an 'expected' mean rank that would result from a
perfectly consistent ranking across regions. Given that there are
twelve regions, eight SEGs, and ten industry divisions, if a perfectly
consistent ranking existed, we would expect the highest paying
region to occupy the first 80 places, in order of relative earnings,
and hence have a mean rank of 851.5. The lowest paying region

Table 9.1 *Relative hourly earnings in Northen Ireland by socio-economic group and industry division, 1972 and 1982, males*

| Industry division | Socio-economic group | | | | | | | (GB) = (100) |
	Managers	Professionals	Intermediate Non-manual	Junior Non-manual	Foremen	Skilled manual	Semi-skilled manual	Unskilled manual
Agriculture	— / *79.1*	— / —	92.4 / —	— / —	115.9 / —	113.9 / *124.2*	130.3 / *123.3*	133.9 / *126.7*
Energy	115.4 / —	89.9 / *100.0*	96.2 / *99.9*	— / —	119.8 / —	107.1 / *92.4*	96.9 / *96.4*	96.5 / *81.4*
Chemicals and metals	— / —	96.7 / —	91.8 / *112.9*	— / —	90.4 / —	88.1 / *75.8*	85.5 / *95.8*	74.2 / *88.1*
Engineering and vehicles	83.8 / *96.0*	95.2 / *94.3*	81.0 / *70.3*	90.4 / *102.4*	89.0 / *94.9*	93.9 / *95.7*	83.2 / *115.2*	87.1 / *110.8*
Other manufacturing	79.9 / *72.2*	58.1 / *77.5*	88.4 / *96.7*	— / *76.4*	89.8 / *86.2*	83.8 / *81.4*	95.1 / *96.5*	91.0 / *95.8*
Construction	83.3 / *121.1*	71.2 / *98.6*	94.3 / *91.7*	— / —	93.2 / *87.3*	88.5 / *87.1*	81.5 / *85.8*	84.6 / *82.1*
Distribution	82.6 / *91.3*	— / —	99.1 / *91.9*	88.4 / *83.8*	81.3 / *99.1*	95.8 / *95.5*	95.9 / *91.6*	95.4 / *92.0*
Transport and communication	110.6 / *74.6*	85.2 / —	97.6 / *94.1*	— / *94.2*	121.0 / —	96.8 / *100.0*	87.6 / *96.1*	85.2 / *81.6*
Business services	77.8 / *74.4*	68.2 / *71.3*	88.4 / *63.1*	— / *85.9*	— / *58.3*	— / —	75.3 / *64.6*	— / —
Other services	84.7 / *128.9*	84.4 / *80.3*	101.3 / *96.9*	98.2 / *122.9*	97.9 / —	94.1 / *85.9*	90.8 / *94.5*	91.8 / *89.7*

Notes: Figures in italics refer to 1982

— = Sample size too small

131

Table 9.2 *Mean ranks of relative earnings by region based on SEGS and industry divisions, 1972 and 1982, males*

Region[a]	Observed mean rank 1972	Observed mean rank 1982	Expected mean rank
GLC	757.6	755.2	851.5
South-East	525.6	532.9	777.5
North-West	505.1	454.9	703.1
West Midlands	484.8	348.6	628.5
Wales	469.2	394.8	554.5
North	434.7	463.6	480.5
Scotland	406.1	559.7	407.5
East Midlands	356.0	345.4	333.5
East Anglia	349.1	375.4	259.5
South-West	345.7	353.7	185.5
Yorks-Humberside	342.0	389.4	111.5
Northern Ireland	302.1	325.2	37.5
χ^2	190.23	189.75	

[a] Rank from highest to lowest on the basis of the first column of data.

Note: the chi-square value refers to the Kruskall–Wallis test of the null hypothesis that there is no significant differences across regions in terms of rankings of relative earnings. For both years, the null hypothesis is rejected at greater than the 0.1 per cent confidence level.

would occupy the last 80 places and its mean rank would be 37.5. Table 9.2 presents the observed and expected mean rank for 1972 and 1982 for males. It shows that each region had several sub-groups (i.e. SEGs/Divisions) with relative earnings that were above or below what we would expect if rankings were perfectly consistent. Hence, the observed and expected series in Table 9.2 do not match all that well. There is considerable bunching of regions around the average, but then this is to be expected since relative earnings are measured against a national average, and dispersion across regions around that average are mostly within about 10 percentage points. Table 9.2 does show that the two regions that are very much at the extremes in terms of relative earnings are Northern Ireland and the GLC, although this is much more the case for the latter region. Also, a chi-squared test of the hypothesis that there is no significant difference between relative earnings

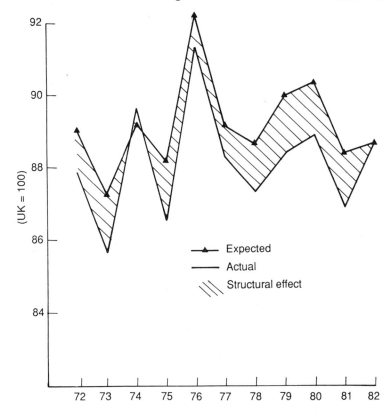

*Figure 9.3 Actual and expected relative earnings in
Northern Ireland (males), 1972-1982*

across regions is rejected (at the 0.1 per cent confidence level).
Finally, it is interesting to note the changes in overall mean
rankings for certain GB regions between 1972 and 1982. For
instance, Scottish earnings moved up significantly, while those in
the West Midlands declined equally as fast.

Company and plant size differences and earnings
Another possible influence on relative earnings might be plant and/
or company size, which is known to be lower in Northern Ireland.
Since there is a positive earnings–size relationship, especially on the
basis of company size, an over-dependence on small units in
Northern Ireland may help to explain the differential in earnings.
Tables 9.3 and 9.4 present the relevant data. They confirm that
there is a positive gradient to the earnings–size relationship,
especially on the basis of company size, and that this gradient

exhibits a steeper slope using Northern Ireland data. The figures also confirm the dependence on smaller units in the province; only about 29 per cent of companies in Northern Ireland employ 5000 or more workers, compared to over 41 per cent in GB (these comparisons are based on the sample sizes for male workers), while the comparable figures for the largest plants are 8.5 and 13.1.

Tables 9.3 and 9.4 show that an earnings differential is apparent for each size-band, which suggests that dependence on smaller units helps to explain only a very small proportion of the overall differential. For males, weighting average weekly pay by the

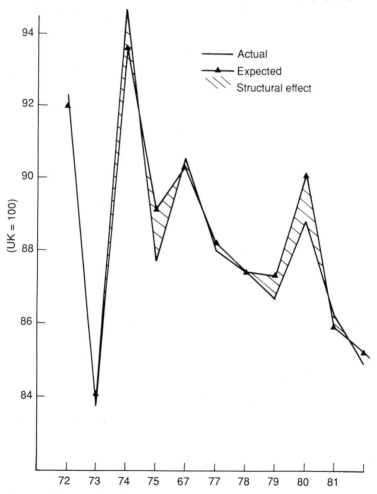

Figure 9.4 Actual and expected relative earnings in Northern Ireland (females), 1972–1982

Table 9.3 Average weekly pay (and sample size) by size of company and sector in Northern Ireland, April 1979ᵃ

Size (employment)	Males			Females		
	Private sector £	Public sector £	Total £	Private sector £	Public sector £	Total £
0-50	81.46 (258)ᶜ	— (0)	81.46 89.56ᵇ (258) (4689)	45.95 (90)	103.50 (3)	47.80 53.95 (93) (1761)
51-99	86.50 (72)	101.10 (9)	88.13 95.06 (81) (1227)	48.37 (30)	— (0)	48.37 54.87 (30) (486)
100-499	89.03 (171)	95.98 (51)	90.63 99.61 (222) (3632)	49.92 (96)	61.77 (27)	52.52 57.05 (123) (1428)
500-999	79.15 (30)	98.55 (9)	83.62 101.98 (39) (1871)	62.42 (39)	117.75 (3)	66.38 59.42 (42) (698)
1000-4999	98.96 (161)	98.56 (162)	98.76 104.84 (323) (4303)	68.21 (82)	77.88 (147)	74.42 62.61 (229) (1729)
5000+	90.81 (60)	102.46 (309)	100.56 104.73 (369) (10976)	44.38 (6)	62.64 (252)	62.22 68.01 (258) (5786)

Source: NES Northern Ireland and GB.

ᵃ Only full-time, no-loss-of-pay, adult workers are included in these figures.

ᵇ Figures in italics refer to comparable all industry data for Great Britain in the same pay-week.

ᶜ Figures in parenthesis refer to the sample size.

percentage of workers in each GB (company) size-band closes the gap in earnings by only 0.5 per cent. The influence of the public sector is given separately for the Northern Ireland data, and this shows that for all size-bands earnings were higher in this sector. It is also apparent that the majority of public sector workers belong to large companies which operate comparatively small plants, and that earnings levels vary by much less, both across company and plant size, when compared to the private sector. Overall, the differential in earnings (for all company and plant sizes) is apparent despite the fact that public sector workers in Northern Ireland are just as highly covered by nationally negotiated collective agreements, and that something in the order of 60 per cent of workers in the private sector work for companies that are based in GB. There is obviously the need for further detailed research to account for these differences.

Table 9.4 *Average weekly pay (and sample size) by size of plant and sector in Northern Ireland, April 1979*[a]

Size (employment)	Males				Females			
	Private sector £	Public sector £	Total £		Private sector £	Public sector £	Total £	
0–50	84.83	98.68	91.42	99.78[b]	52.59	68.19	62.98	63.47
	(552)[c]	(501)	(1053)	(18910)	(222)	(443)	(665)	(9680)
51–99	89.23	—	89.23	95.58	49.71	—	49.71	52.43
	(43)	(0)	(43)	(609)	(27)	(0)	(27)	(216)
100–199	84.46	—	84.46	96.89	52.98	—	52.98	54.53
	(58)	(0)	(58)	(878)	(42)	(0)	(42)	(352)
200–499	91.93	103.23	92.38	98.23	53.78	—	53.78	57.18
	(73)	(3)	(76)	(1610)	(42)	(0)	(42)	(595)
500–999	89.82	—	89.82	101.63	58.74	—	58.74	61.20
	(45)	(0)	(45)	(1204)	(32)	(0)	(32)	(391)
1000+	112.20	116.10	114.07	108.75	70.13	58.87	69.01	66.56
	(62)	(57)	(119)	(3487)	(27)	(3)	(30)	(654)

Source: NES Northern Ireland and GB.

[a] Only full-time, no-loss-of-pay, adult workers are included in these figures.

[b] Figures in italics refer to comparable all industry data for Great Britain in the same pay-week.

[c] Figures in parenthesis refer to the sample size.

The collective bargaining structure in Northern Ireland

Institutional factors may help to explain relative earnings differentials, especially if wages are not set on the basis of local labour market conditions but rather by collective bargaining dominated by nationally negotiated agreements. The latter is consistent with the 'wage-leadership' hypothesis (e.g. Hart and MacKay, 1977) that earnings changes in a leading market (viz. the South-East regional labour market), determined by excess demand for labour, are passed on, in whole or in part, to lagging markets. This hypothesis, therefore, predicts that inter-regional wage differentials will tend to be eliminated the stronger is this wage transmission process.

In Northern Ireland, the importance of institutional factors in determining earnings can be considered by (i) comparing the differing bargaining structures that existed in the province and the UK; and (ii) by estimating wage equations that take into account the 'wage-leadership' mechanism. It is also worth noting that over the period of the 1960s and early 1970s, trade unions may have played an important role in the process of regional earnings convergence (whereby earnings in Northern Ireland caught up from being 81.8 per cent of the UK average in 1961 to 94.9 per cent in 1976) in at least three ways: first, through the establishment of formal 'parity' agreements within the rapidly expanding public sector in Northern Ireland; secondly, because of a move away from local industry agreements to national agreements (Black, 1985b: 29–30, gives extensive evidence for the period 1952–84 of UK agreements superseding Northern Ireland based industry agreements); and thirdly, through 'take-overs' of local private sector industry by multi-site organizations (with headquarters mainly in GB) and the establishment of *large* 'branch-plants' in sectors such as Textiles, Vehicles, Rubber and Plastics. Hence, given the opportunity, trade unions appear to have negotiated pay levels compatible to other (large) plants located outside Northern Ireland. Direct evidence is not available to corroborate this assertion, although it is interesting to note that *relative* earnings grew faster, between 1961 and 1976, in such sectors as Textiles, Rubber and Plastics (Other Manufacturing), Bricks, Pottery and Glass, Vehicles and the Food and Drink industries, all of which experienced substantial inward investment in the 1960s and early 1970s.

Turning now to consider the relative collective bargaining structures, Table 9.5 sets out the basic figures for bargaining coverage (including type) and average hourly earnings for male full-time adult workers at industry level. The figures in italics refer to Great Britain; the figures in brackets refer to 1984 (in Northern Ireland's case) or 1985 (for Great Britain). Overall in Northern Ireland, coverage for males by collective agreement was high (over 70 per cent) with the most important types of agreement involving a national bargaining structure. Industries with above-average coverage levels were typically in the public sector (Energy and Water, Construction, Transport and Communications and Other Services), while the high coverage figure for Engineering and Vehicles includes a sizeable number of employees working in companies held in public ownership (e.g. Harland and Wolff, and Short Bros. and Harland). National plus supplementary[3] bargaining was particularly dominant in Energy and Water, Engineering and Vehicles (although not by 1984), and to a lesser extent Other Manufacturing industries. Over the period covered there was a

Table 9.5 Coverage by collective agreement (males) by industry in Northern Ireland and Great Britain 1973 and 1984/5

Industry (1980 Division)		Average hourly earnings £	Any collective agreement	Percentage covered by National plus supplementary agreement	National agreement only	Supplementary agreement only
All industries	(0–9)	0.84(3.83) *0.91(4.53)*	70.1(75.2) *74.0(64.2)*	35.1(14.2) *23.7(14.5)*	27.0(46.5) *40.3(37.7)*	8.0(14.5) *10.0(12.0)*
Agriculture, etc.	(0)	0.76 – *0.63(2.65)*	55.3(11.1) *41.5(38.9)*	29.0(0.0) *13.9(7.08)*	2.6(0.0) *22.0(28.8)*	23.7(11.1) *5.6(3.0)*
Energy and water	(1)	1.13(4.60) *1.00(5.03)*	100.0(100.0) *96.4(90.4)*	84.6(85.2) *12.5(15.9)*	15.4(14.8) *81.3(69.9)*	0.0(0.0) *2.6(4.8)*
Metals and chemicals	(2)	0.93(3.25) *0.98(4.70)*	62.5(32.3) *71.6(61.0)*	12.5(6.5) *37.7(23.3)*	20.8(9.7) *19.6(12.3)*	29.2(16.1) *14.4(25.4)*
Engineering and vehicles	(3)	0.84(3.73) *0.97(4.46)*	93.2(80.2) *76.4(56.5)*	82.2(12.6) *44.4(20.8)*	9.6(19.0) *18.4(13.7)*	1.4(48.6) *13.4(22.0)*
Other manufacturing	(4)	0.78(3.31) *0.93(4.38)*	59.4(66.3) *66.8(57.0)*	32.8(27.5) *24.3(17.5)*	10.9(15.3) *25.9(19.7)*	15.6(23.5) *16.6(19.9)*
Construction	(5)	0.74(3.02) *0.89(3.90)*	76.8(64.9) *80.5(66.3)*	44.6(17.5) *21.9(16.8)*	32.1(45.6) *55.8(46.8)*	0.0(1.8) *2.8(2.6)*
Distribution	(6)	0.75(3.00) *0.82(3.82)*	23.7(47.4) *45.0(33.9)*	13.6(7.0) *10.5(6.2)*	3.4(16.7) *22.3(17.3)*	6.8(23.7) *12.3(10.4)*
Transport and communications	(7)	0.82(3.82) *0.91(4.36)*	91.2(93.1) *87.7(83.0)*	20.6(1.7) *14.5(9.7)*	47.1(92.8) *63.4(60.1)*	23.5(8.6) *9.8(13.1)*
Business services	(8)	1.05(4.53) *1.26(6.14)*	18.8(65.4) *40.6(37.5)*	0.0(0.0) *9.9(7.7)*	12.5(57.7) *16.6(19.2)*	6.3(7.7) *14.1(10.6)*
Other services	(9)	0.91(4.13) *1.09(5.00)*	87.1(91.4) *87.7(90.3)*	23.9(4.3) *13.3(14.4)*	63.2(86.3) *72.5(74.5)*	0.0(0.8) *2.0(1.4)*

Source: New earning surveys NI and GB.

Notes: Figures in italics refer to Great Britain. Figures in brackets refer to 1984 (Northern Ireland) and 1985 (Great Britain).

Table 9.6 Coverage by collective agreement (females) by industry in Northern Ireland and Great Britain 1973 and 1984-8

Industry (1980 Division)		Average hourly earnings £	Any collective agreement	Percentage covered by National plus supplementary agreement	National agreement only	Supplementary agreement only
All industries	(0-9)	0.52(2.77) *0.60(3.34)*	62.5(80.7) *66.4(64.0)*	22.4(7.7) *14.0(10.4)*	35.2(64.3) *44.1(45.8)*	4.9(8.7) *8.3(7.8)*
Agriculture,	(0)	0.57 – *0.44 –*	78.6 – *29.9 –*	50.0 – *10.3 –*	7.1 – *12.4 –*	21.4 – *7.2 –*
Energy and water	(1)	0.57(3.04) *0.66(4.01)*	100.0(100.0) *93.2(83.1)*	100.0(88.9) *17.5(27.8)*	0.0(11.1) *72.7(52.0)*	0.0(0.0) *3.1(3.3)*
Metals and chemicals	(2)	0.56(2.15) *0.55(3.19)*	0.0(20.0) *51.4(46.6)*	0.0(20.0) *19.6(13.0)*	0.0(0.0) *16.4(9.3)*	0.0(0.0) *15.5(24.3)*
Engineering and vehicles	(3)	0.53(2.91) *0.55(2.99)*	92.9(71.4) *68.8(46.4)*	78.6(42.9) *37.8(16.5)*	14.3(28.6) *18.2(8.4)*	0.0(0.0) *12.8(21.5)*
Other manufacturing	(4)	0.43(2.20) *0.53(2.82)*	45.3(68.7) *60.7(53.3)*	20.3(17.9) *18.8(14.7)*	12.5(17.9) *27.2(22.8)*	12.5(32.8) *14.7(15.8)*
Construction	(5)	0.47(2.51) *0.55(2.98)*	0.0(25.0) *24.2(16.8)*	0.0(0.0) *3.7(2.8)*	0.0(25.0) *9.9(11.0)*	0.0(0.0) *16.5(3.0)*
Distribution	(6)	0.39(2.07) *0.47(2.61)*	13.2(34.3) *38.5(36.5)*	7.9(5.7) *8.3(5.0)*	0.0(8.6) *19.6(21.5)*	5.3(20.0) *10.6(9.9)*
Transport and communications	(7)	0.57(2.98) *0.67(3.60)*	100.0(81.3) *78.5(70.4)*	0.0(0.0) *5.3(4.7)*	100.0(81.3) *64.9(54.3)*	0.0(0.0) *8.1(11.3)*
Business services	(8)	0.55(3.37) *0.66(3.70)*	9.1(68.4) *47.3(37.6)*	0.0(2.6) *11.7(8.1)*	9.1(57.9) *26.6(21.6)*	0.0(7.9) *9.7(7.8)*
Other services	(9)	0.60(2.92) *0.75(3.71)*	87.8(96.4) *87.3(89.9)*	20.8(1.8) *7.8(10.7)*	67.0(93.2) *77.5(78.3)*	0.0(1.4) *2.0(0.9)*

Notes: Figures in italics refer to Great Britain. Figures in brackets refer to 1984 (Northern Ireland) and 1985 (Great Britain). – Sample size too small.

139

Table 9.7 *Percentage of male employees covered by collective agreements in certain groups in Northern Ireland in 1973 and 1984*

| Employment Group (SEG/DIV) | National only | % covered by collective agreement | | Not covered by agreement |
		National and supplementary	Supplementary only	
Other manufacturing	10.9 (15.3)	32.8 (27.5)	15.6 (23.5)	40.6 (33.7)
Transport and communication	47.1 (92.8)	20.6 (1.7)	23.5 (8.6)	8.8 (6.9)
Other services	63.2 (86.3)	23.9 (4.3)	0.0 (0.8)	12.9 (8.6)
Skilled Manual (6)				
Other manufacturing (4)	26.2 (65.3)	21.4 (15.3)	19.1 (6.9)	33.3 (12.5)
Transport and communication (7)	5.3 (38.5)	84.2 (53.8)	5.3 (7.7)	5.2 (0.0)
Other services (9)	9.1 (0.0)	86.4 (75.0)	0.0 (0.0)	4.5 (25.0)
Unskilled Manual (8)				
Other manufacturing (4)	25.0 (50.0)	12.5 (10.0)	37.5 (0.0)	25.0 (40.0)
Transport and communication (7)	33.3 (na)	0.0 (na)	66.6 (na)	0.0 (na)
Other services (9)	5.1 (15.9)	89.7 (71.0)	2.6 (0.0)	2.6 (13.0)

Source: New Earnings Survey.

Notes: Figures in parenthesis refer to 1984.

na = not available.

move towards national agreements only, which is likely to have enhanced any 'wage transmission' mechanism (cf. the Construction, Transport and Communications, Business Services and Other Services industries). Nevertheless, the collective bargaining structure placed a good deal of emphasis on company and plant bargaining to supplement Northern Ireland and UK industry-wide agreements, and it is likely (given recent evidence for Great Britain) that supplementary bargaining was the most important feature of the bargaining process. Hence, whilst most agreements involved some national bargaining, which tends to set a wage-floor, the institutional forces determining pay left quite a lot of room to supplementary bargains that were probably more responsive to local labour market conditions.

The comparable figures on collective bargaining for females are given in Table 9.6. These show that female coverage was lower than male coverage in 1973, but grew four times faster between 1973 and 1984. The overall pattern is very similar to that for males, except that female full-time employment is very small in the Energy and Water, Metals and Chemicals, Construction and Transport and Communications industries, which explains the relative differences for these industries. This is also the reason for the smaller proportion across all industries of female workers covered by single-employer agreements. Finally, it is worth noting that, as with the bargaining structures for males, national-only and supplementary-only agreements were also higher in Northern Ireland by 1984, the former because of the 'Other Services' sector, and the latter because of Other Manufacturing and Distribution.

Hence, the overall picture suggests that nationally negotiated wage agreements played a significant role in determining wages in the Province, but that there was also substantial room for 'local conditions' to have an influence. To go beyond conjecture requires an attempt at explicitly modelling the processes that determine wages. As an illustration of the type of results that can be obtained, we have estimated Phillips-type wage equations for three industries, and for two occupation groups within those industries. If the 'wage-leadership' hypothesis has any validity at all, then we should expect to find some evidence in its favour from these results. Before presenting the model, it is useful to consider the bargaining structures for these industries (Table 9.7). This shows that in Other Manufacturing there were substantial numbers not covered by collective aggreements, and so for these workers we might expect less of a role for 'wage-leadership'. In both the other industries, there was a growth in national-only bargaining, although the two occupation groups chosen from these industries were dominated by a two-tier bargaining structure. Hence, we have a cross-section of

Table 9.8 Regression results for the wage equations

Employment group	Estimated values of coefficients					ρ	R^2	$\bar{R}^2$	DW
	α	β_1	β_2	β_3	β_4				
Other manufacturing	0.12 (2.3)	0.75 (2.6)	-0.61 (1.7)	0.20 (2.8)	0.34 (1.8)	—	0.90	0.82	2.2
Transport and communication	0.08 (0.7)	0.81 (1.7)	-0.63 (0.8)	0.17 (1.1)	0.63 (1.6)	—	0.82	0.68	1.7
Other services	-0.06 (0.4)	0.33 (0.5)	1.17 (1.4)	-0.12 (0.8)	0.76 (1.3)	-0.93 (9.5)	0.84	0.72	2.4
Skilled manual									
Other manufacturing	0.05 (0.9)	0.72 (1.9)	-0.39 (0.9)	0.11 (1.2)	0.71 (3.3)	-0.83 (3.9)	0.95	0.91	1.8
Transport and communication	0.03 (0.4)	1.13 (1.7)	—	-0.13 (0.7)	0.77 (1.5)	—	0.51	0.27	2.5
Other services	-0.06 (0.4)	0.59 (1.2)	0.22 (0.2)	-0.01 (0.07)	1.13 (2.1)	—	0.77	0.59	2.1
Unskilled manual									
Other manufacturing	-0.01 (0.1)	1.10 (1.5)	—	0.18 (1.7)	0.80 (2.9)	-0.55 (1.9)	0.77	0.66	2.6
Transport and communication	-0.12 (1.6)	1.62 (1.7)	—	-0.19 (1.1)	1.73 (3.5)	-0.60 (2.0)	0.81	0.71	2.5
Other services	0.06 (0.7)	-0.11 (0.2)	-0.33 (0.7)	0.07 (0.7)	0.68 (1.6)	-0.71 (3.0)	0.89	0.77	3.0

Note: The model estimated was:

$$\log\left(\frac{W_t}{W_{t-1}}\right) = \alpha + \beta_1 \log\left(\frac{rW_t^N}{rW_{t-1}^N}\right)$$

$$+ \beta_2 U_t + \beta_3 \log\left(\frac{U_t}{U_{t-1}}\right) + \beta_4 \log\left(\frac{P_t}{P_{t-1}}\right)$$

Where W = nominal hourly earnings (excluding overtime)

rW^N = real hourly earnings (excluding overtime) in Great Britain

U = unemployment rate in Northern Ireland

P = Northern Ireland consumer price index.

t-values in parenthesis

α = rho (first-order autoregressive parameter).

bargaining structures which should provide a potentially diverse set of results.

The model estimated is shown in Table 9.8. Basically, local labour market conditions have been included via the unemployment variables (as is standard in this type of model), while the other two major influences on nominal wage growth are consumer price inflation and real wage growth in the nation. The latter is included to take account of 'institutional forces' that transmit wage gains in other labour markets to the Northern Ireland market-place. The model was estimated by ordinary least squares[5] and a correction was used where necessary for first-order serial correlation of the residuals.

Our prior expectations are for a negative sign on the unemployment variable, a positive sign for the growth of unemployment, and price expectations (proxied by actual price inflation) near to 1. In the event, the unemployment variables provided a mixed set of parameter estimates, with perverse (and often statistically insignificant) results.[6] The estimates of the parameters of the expected rate of inflation are plausible (and significant), although for the Other Manufacturing equation the value is rather low (which contrasts with the results for manual workers in this industry). Of most interest are the estimates of β_1, which are generally positive and significant. Only for unskilled manual workers in the Other Services industry is there no evidence to support the wage transmission process. The latter effect was also relatively weaker for skilled manual employees working in the same industry, which suggests that high levels of two-tier bargaining for both these groups may account for these results. The hypothesis being tested is particularly vindicated in the Transport and Communications industry, where National Only aggreements became more important over time, bringing the Northern Ireland bargaining structure into line with that existing in the rest of the UK.[7] In conclusion, these early results do tend to show that real wage gains in the GB labour market were transmitted in whole or in part to workers in Northern Ireland. It is now necessary to extend the analysis to other occupations, industries and regions, while at the same time using the underlying figures available within the data-set to help interpret the results.

Conclusions

It has been possible to use earnings data for Northern Ireland to show that any relative differences in wage levels with Great Britain are not due to an over-dependence on low-paying industries, nor are they due to the size of companies or plants in the province. While these factors may play some role, the estimates produced show that it is quantifiably small. In contrast, wages do seem to be strongly influenced by the gains negotiated by workers in Great Britain and then transmitted through national bargaining agreements to the Northern Ireland labour market. This may account for the convergence of earnings towards the United Kingdom average in recent decades, a process that has occurred despite continuing disparities in unemployment rates between the different parts of the United Kingdom. The results produced so far are, however, tentative since much more needs to be done in making use of what is a unique data-base of earnings in the spatial economies of the United Kingdon.

Notes

1. The data on regional cost of living indices are taken from Reward Regional Surveys (1987). The data only go back to 1973, and have been converted to a 1975 base. The relative difference in the cost of living was based on the most recent survey for January 1987, when average prices in Northern Ireland were 89 per cent of the UK average, while relative average prices in the other regions were as follows: GLC = 133 per cent, South-East=109 per cent, and East Anglia = 96 per cent.

2. Actual relative earnings are calculated as $\dfrac{\Sigma e_i w_i}{\Sigma e_i} \Big/ \dfrac{\Sigma_i^N w_i^N}{\Sigma e_i^N}$

where e represents the number of employees; i the industry (split into ten groupings) in the province, while a superscript N represents the industry at the national level; w represents average hourly wages. 'Expected' relative earnings are calculated as:

$$\frac{\Sigma[e_i w_i] \, (e_i^N/e_i)}{\Sigma e_i^N} \Bigg/ \frac{\Sigma_i^N w_i^N}{\Sigma e_i^N}$$

where it can be seen that the latter amounts to average earnings that would have occurred in the province if it had had the national distribution of employment across industries, and Northern Ireland wage levels. Note, it is also possible to weight Northern Ireland's earnings by occupational (i.e. SEG) employment. Similar results are obtained whichever approach is used.

3. Supplementary bargaining covers company (all plants), district (some plants) and local (one-plant) agreements.
4. Note, data were available for the period 1972-82. All variables are for the sub-group estimated, except that there were no breakdowns available for the unemployment and consumer price indices.
5. The structural equation for GB would be the same as for Northern Ireland, except that GB real wage growth would obviously be omitted. Hence, we are assuming that local labour market conditions, and price expectations, set GB wage growth which is then transmitted (in *ex post* real terms) to the Northern Ireland market. Hence, it would be statistically preferable to estimate Northern Ireland and GB wage equations together as a system (using Zellner's Least Squares), to include any cross-product covariances of the error structures of the two equations. This has not yet been attempted, and so our results may lack efficiency.
6. The positive value for the unemployment rate variable in the Other Service equation probably reflects the fact that over this period as unemployment grew in the province, this industry was instrumental in 'soaking up' some of the newly unemployed.
7. There is evidence that wage levels in this industry went through a process of rapid growth in the early to mid-1970s, which helps to explain the parameter estimates obtained for β^1.

References

Black J.B.H. (1985a) 'Regional Earnings Covergence: the Case of Northern Ireland', *Regional Studies*, 19(6), 1-8.

Black, J.B.H. (1985b) 'Collective Bargaining Structure in Northern Ireland', mimeo.

Hart, R.A. and D.I. Mackay (1977) 'Wage Inflation, Regional Policy and the Regional Earnings Structure', *Economica*, 44, 267-81.

Reward Regional Surveys (1987) 'Cost of Living', Reward Regional Surveys Ltd.

PART IV
URBAN COMMUNITIES
AND SOCIAL POLICY

10 Community-based planning and development in Northern Ireland: the case of Community Technical Aid
Tim Blackman and Joe Larkin

> we require a dynamic conception of how to *optimise* basic need satisfaction given the *best understanding* but *without* engaging in cultural imperialism or the dogmatic imposition of expertise. (Doyal and Gough, 1984: 22)

This chapter is concerned with how struggles about the built environment gave rise to a new resource for community groups in Northern Ireland. Our starting point is the contribution to welfare debate by Doyal and Gough (1984). They argue that certain preconditions are necessary for people to be able to express needs that can be rationally defended. Popular understanding of technical issues, freely available methodological skills and the minimizing of vested interests are three essential preconditions. For many community groups in deprived areas this has boiled down to getting practical help to back up local projects and campaigns. With these preconditions fulfilled, people can plan for their needs and undertake action for necessary changes, rather than be disabled by lack of knowledge, skills or means of exposing vested interests. Planning based on popular participation would, Doyal and Gough argue, enable protection against tyranny by others, the production of better policies by involving those affected by decisions, encourage self-development and the capacity for critical judgement, and guarantee the equal dignity of all citizens. They present these arguments as a programme for both debate and action.

These aspirations are radical and utopian, but one field where the ideas have been influential is planning and architecture. Concepts such as public participation in planning, planning aid, popular planning, community architecture and community technical aid reflect this influence (see for example Skeffington, 1969; Sewell and Coppock, 1977; Curtis and Edwards, 1980; Boaden, Goldsmith, Hampton and Stringer, 1982; Gardiner, Crook and Gomilny, 1982; Newham Docklands Forum, 1983; Kirkham, 1983; Hester, 1984; Evans, 1985; Woolley, 1985). More recently economic development has incorporated these ideas, with the rise of community business, local co-ops and small economic projects (see, for example, Collective Design/Projects, 1985; Centre for Employment Initiatives, 1985; McArthur, 1986; Buchanon, 1986; Robertson, 1986; Goodwin and Duncan, 1986; Gaffikin and Morrissey, 1986).

On the one hand, such approaches are open to criticism as means of accommodating or managing community action so that it does not develop into political challenges on centres of power (for example, Byrne, 1986). On the other hand, those involved often view these initiatives as movements for local control, prefiguring at local level what is not yet possible at larger scales where the interests of private capital or state bureaucracies dominate (for example, Blunkett and Green, 1983). However what appears particularly significant to us about these developments is the aspect of breaking down the separation between people with specialist expertise and knowledge from the people who need such skills but cannot get them. This obviously echoes Illich's critique of the disabling professions (Illich et al., 1977), although we do not see 'enabling' as a solution to housing and planning problems, but as a strategy in diverse struggles to meet human needs in the face of radical and systematic inequalities. While many people lack the power to control their lives, they are further disabled by a lack of structures to do anything about it.

This chapter results from a two-year research project funded by the Economic and Social Research Council between November 1984 and November 1986 which studied an organization specifically established to provide enabling resources to community groups, Community Technical Aid (CTA). This was not a government initiative, but one that came from the grassroots to meet widely perceived needs in many localities throughout Northern Ireland.

Technical aid
In Britain 'planning aid' developed from the late 1960s to help local people understand planning structures and processes, develop their own planning proposals and participate effectively at public inquiries. 'Technical aid' came about a little later to assist self-help and community groups' own planning and development activities. Woolley (1987) describes the growth of community technical aid from the mid 1970s as a movement for 'user control' of environmental professionals. The Association of Community Technical Aid Centres (1985), or ACTAC, locates the origins of technical aid in the unavailability or unsuitability of technical support for community groups taking advantage of growing state funding for local projects in the 1970s, stating: 'The mid-1970s saw an explosion of voluntary sector initiatives which had one thing in

common – the need to convert or use a building or waste land for community benefit' (Association of Community Technical Aid Centres, 1985: 2). What happened was the development of grant-aided centres providing community groups with the services of architects and planners to help with funding applications for these initiatives and work on implementation. There are many different types, and some are essentially private practices, but we refer to them under the general title of community technical aid centres.

ACTAC argue that the growth of the voluntary sector in this area has been a response both to the failures of the state to deliver effective and suitable services and facilities, and to the lack of skill and know-how available to enable community groups to put ideas for improvements to the environment into practice.

From our own research we would qualify this view. These 'voluntary sector' initiatives have been highly dependent on state support. They may easily be used to reduce the size of the public sector for political reasons and to reduce total resources being invested in public services and facilities (as has happened with many local councils in Britain which have taken much bigger losses from central government rate support grant cutbacks than gains from Urban Programme funds). In addition, failures of a particular kind of state should not be seen as a failure of the concept of state provision itself. Woolley (1987) suggests from his experience that there is much more potential for a partnership between community technical aid and the public sector than for a partnership with the private sector, where commercial criteria dominate.

The possibility of progressive local government practice in this area in Northern Ireland is very slim. Conservative civil servants dominate the local state, and elected local government is bereft of major functions and powers. Community groups have not been able to enrol the assistance of state professionals. The cooperation of planners in Northern Ireland is constrained by the Official Secrets Act because they are civil servants.

The reason for the establishment of Community Technical Aid (Northern Ireland) is spelt out in a booklet published by the Northern Ireland Technical Aid Group (1983). It states that:

> The policies and practices of planning, housing and transport authorities have often been criticised for threatening community life in many parts of the Province and for involving high social costs, such as blight and uncertainty, the destruction of local economies and neighbourhoods, and loss of population.

The booklet argues for 'popular planning' as an alternative, claiming that:

The lack of technical advice, assistance and resources in the Province has consistently inhibited local community groups in tackling projects such as developing vacant land and buildings, bringing forward proposals to improve their areas or creating socially useful jobs. This is a major gap in the provisions of services to promote community development in Northern Ireland.

The argument was that many people, particularly in deprived areas, were excluded from full and effective participation in their localities, and that particular skills and resources were required by community groups (assuming such organization occurs) to enable participation: to bring forward people's own plans, to identify causes of problems and solutions to them, and to penetrate official discourse and bureaucratic secrecy. A fundamental problem in this respect was that the vast majority of professionals and 'experts' were enrolled by the state or by private institutions; Morrison (1986) estimates that some 70 per cent of professional planners in Northern Ireland are employed by the Department of the Environment and most of the rest work in private practice which is largely dependent on commissions from government agencies.

It is people who are least able to do anything about it who get trapped in the worst housing areas or faced with the most destructive effects of recession, cuts or discrimination. Taking action from a local base to improve social conditions is a frustrating and difficult task. What happens in a particular locality has become increasingly determined by institutions and centres of power which are not place-bound. In Northern Ireland the problem is intensified by Direct Rule, which means that government bodies are only really accountable *upwards* to ministers. The main reason for the removal of local government powers, which of course has been occurring throughout the UK as the central state finds it necessary to govern localities directly, was sectarian conflict. While some people might be happy with a situation of government by a pyramid of quangos it seems important to continue to search for ways of empowering social groups so that there is at least means of establishing popular control over the created environments of their localities, even though this may mean accepting the sectarian geography of some areas. The struggle for such means is an interesting one in Northern Ireland. It has involved a range of initiatives in the non-governmental or 'voluntary' sector since the late 1960s, and one of the most recent of these is the Community Technical Aid project.

Research strategy and methods

In summary, our research strategy was to monitor CTA at three levels. Internal monitoring involved investigating the organization's structure, functioning and work through participant observation (and a degree of action research), semi-structured interviews and the use of written records, reports, correspondence, etc. Member-level monitoring involved a postal questionnaire survey of the 84 groups which used CTA from establishment in January 1984 to October/November 1985 (response rate 42 per cent), complemented by four case studies. External monitoring involved six postal questionnaire surveys: (i) all the 539 community groups registered in various community indexes for Northern Ireland (response rate 32 per cent); (ii) 50 per cent of the 1180 environmental professionals in the public and private sectors listed by the professional institutes for planners, architects, landscape architects, surveyors and civil engineers in Northern Ireland (response rate 54 per cent); (iii) all the 26 District Councils (response rate 77 per cent); (iv) all five main political parties (response rate 100 per cent); (v) all 43 Northern Ireland Housing Executive District Managers (response rate 86 per cent); and (vi) all seven Divisional Planning and Development Officers of the Department of the Environment for Northern Ireland (response rate 75 per cent).

We also investigated the context of CTA (in addition to the external monitoring) by drawing upon existing literature, visiting similar centres and attending conferences in Britain, and organizing an international conference on community-based planning and development held in Belfast in September 1986 (Blackman, 1987). In total 40 interviews were conducted and taped, and a large collection of written and photographic material was built up. A video was made to disseminate results of the project and the issues it raises to community groups.

The context of CTA

One of the founding members of CTA, a community worker in West Belfast, told us in an interview:

> A community group often has its own set of interests, its own criteria and its own needs to meet which are often totally different from those of the relevant public bodies. In this situation the community group has a right to express its own interests, its own criteria and identify its own needs in a professional and positive manner.

This call for establishing an equal relationship in terms of access to professional skills and knowledge between community groups and the state was at the forefront of the move to establish CTA. The initiative came from a small group of community workers and academics who concluded from their experiences that an important reason why community associations failed to achieve their aims was a lack of technical know-how and technical credibility. This small group was largely unaware of the technical and planning aid movement in Britain. Their experiences were mainly in the areas of redevelopment and housing struggles in Belfast. It was against this background that a public conference was held in Magee College, Derry, in May 1983 to learn about planning and technical aid in Britain and to consider a proposal to establish this type of service in Northern Ireland.

The proceedings of this conference were later submitted as written evidence to the Inquiry held by the Environment Committee of the Northern Ireland Assembly into the Housing Executive's controversial *Belfast Housing Renewal Strategy*, along with the proposal to establish a technical aid centre (Northern Ireland Assembly, 1983). This led to substantial backing for such a centre from the Assembly until its demise in 1986. Interestingly, the Housing Executive Board also expressed support when it agreed to grant aid CTA at an early stage – a decision which, however, was blocked by the Department of the Environment (NI) which itself assumed the role of sole central government source of funds for the organization.

The initiators of CTA assumed that housing, particularly housing defects and redevelopment, and community plans would be the main areas of need. To examine more systematically the nature of local needs and the activities of community groups we undertook a series of surveys of community groups in Northern Ireland. The most common areas of community action were play facilities and recreation. Other common areas were Housing Executive (public sector) housing and environmental improvements.

We asked respondents about standards of provision in their localities. Play facilities and employment came bottom of the list. Environmental improvements, recreation, transport and community education also fared badly. We also asked about opportunities for the public to influence decisions. Views on this tended to be similar to views on standards of provision in those areas, suggesting a positive link between the two. A notable exception was Housing Executive housing, where over 40 per cent of groups responding considered opportunities for participation to be bad, while only 12 per cent considered standards of provision to be bad. We found a clear disagreement between Housing Executive District Managers and community groups about opportunities for public participation in Housing Executive decisions, with only one of the 37 managers who responded stating that such opportunities were bad.

The major activities of the 32 community groups that had used CTA and which responded to our survey in October–November 1985 were generally similar to non-users: mostly Housing Executive housing, environmental improvements, play facilities and recreation. However, private housing and employment appeared as major activities among CTA user groups, reflecting areas where technical input can be very important, e.g. housing renewal and building conversion, and thus CTA involvement more likely than in some other activities. The main difference between this population and non-users was that user-groups tended to be disproportionately concentrated in Greater Belfast rather than the (more rural or small town) rest of Northern Ireland.

The development of CTA
CTA is a small non-governmental organization for Northern Ireland formed in January 1984 to provide professional advice and assistance for community and tenants' associations working with technical problems of housing, planning and the built environment. There are several 'umbrella' organizations in Northern Ireland providing services to community associations and taking up issues of concern to socially deprived groups. CTA filled a gap in what those other organizations provided.

The organization built up a varied membership of tenants' and residents' associations, community development and resource groups, housing associations, environmental groups, mother and toddler groups, youth and recreation groups, women's organizations and interested individuals. There was considerable turnover in membership, but not of Board members. On the one hand, this gave continuity, but it also reflected limited interest among community groups in getting involved in managing CTA.

CTA attracted sufficient funding during 1983 to be able to employ a Development Officer on 1 January 1984 on a two-year contract. The first grant received by CTA was from the Joseph Rowntree Memorial Trust for three years in cooperation with the Northern Ireland Volunatry Trust. Rowntree also made available funds to pay consultants to advise CTA in its first stages. Belfast City Council, influenced by the controversy about the *Belfast Housing Renewal Strategy* also made a grant over three years from non-renewable Belfast Areas of Need funds. Further grants were made by the Gulbenkian Foundation and the Ireland Fund. The Department of the Environment for Northern Ireland made a grant over two years in response to the Northern Ireland Assembly's report referred to above. All of these sources envisaged their support as initial seeding finance and this totalled £130,000. In addition, two district councils outside Belfast gave some financial support to CTA for projects carried out in their areas, and one gave a small general grant.

CTA-fund raised as a pilot project – the way to demonstrate a need was to provide the service – but whilst fund-raising initially went well, the limitation of funding commitments to seeding grants soon became a cause of financial insecurity and caused difficulty in filling technical posts (the Development Officer was a community worker – probably an inappropriate appointment). This problem of attracting and keeping suitable technical staff appeared to be unique to CTA, as we discovered no such situation in technical and planning aid centres we visited in Britain. It appeared that given the domination of environmental professionals' employment by a few state bodies in Northern Ireland working for CTA was perceived as risky in terms of both job security and career prospects.

CTA had to commission private architects to make progress on its first projects, mainly for community groups resisting redevelopment in Belfast, Larne and Carrickfergus. Difficulties with getting organized as a technical service continued for several months.

CTA entered a new, much more stable phase with the appointment in October 1985 of an Architect/Project Officer who moved from private practice. He was complemented by three appointments made using the government's Action for Community Employment (ACE) scheme: two technicians and a secretary. These appointments can only be for 12–18 months, raising similar problems of turnover experienced by technical and planning aid centres in Britain which use staff employed through MSC schemes. A second architect was appointed in January 1987 following a fund raising drive.

The organization's efforts to secure further grant-aid from trusts met with a poor response during 1985 and 1986, and indications were that trusts expected the organization to be core-funded by government by this stage. In October 1985 CTA approached the Department of the Environment (NI) to grant-aid 75 per cent of core running costs, estimated at £117,000 for 1986/87, for three years. Several months passed without any decision, and CTA organized a lobby involving prominent organizations and individuals and the main political parties to try to get a decision. Statements of support were forthcoming from many quarters and after a delay of nine months, during which there appeared to be indecision about whether to fund CTA and which caused the organization considerable financial difficulties, the Minister agreed to further grant-aid. In a letter to CTA's Secretary, an official stated:

You should be aware that the Minister, Mr Needham, has received a substantial number of letters from public and other representatives supporting the case for further funding of CTA and that this cross-community support is, and should continue to be a most important feature of the work of the organization.

This did not solve CTA's financial problems, but it did enable its continuing survival, although on a small scale. CTA still has to search for other means of generating income.

CTA's work

CTA's work can be classified into three categories: problem-solving; projects; and issues and education.

CTA received a large amount of requests from community groups which involved 'problem-solving': visits to assess dampness, settlement, structural defects, heating system malfunctions, building standards and planning applications, and to give independent technical advice and back-up to community action about these problems. There have been a number of successful interventions by CTA in this area.

Projects, on the other hand, cover a less wide range but require greater staff time and often design work. The first project requests involved community groups in redevelopment areas in Belfast, Larne and Carrickfergus who wanted to oppose redevelopment and draw up their own plans for area improvement. As noted above, CTA commissioned private consultants on these projects due to a lack of in-house technical staff. The main effect of their intervention has been to scale down clearance proposals to minimize local disruption.

We made three case studies of these projects. There was a high degree of satisfaction with CTA's role among the community groups, but a more circumspect approach to its intervention among Housing Executive officials. The Regional Director involved in the Larne project considered that CTA was an obstacle to improving housing conditions there. In Bloomfield, East Belfast, the District Manager took the view that while CTA was a good thing, it could be led into supporting impossible cases:

CTA has a positive role to play. It can inform people of policies, technical information, physical and financial constraints. It can grasp community views on building design and translate them into technical jargon . . . . But CTA were involved by Bloomfield Residents' Association for the wrong reasons – to bludgeon the Housing Executive. I think the whole area should be redeveloped. My primary concern is that building gets moving.

In fact, we found that CTA rarely supported a community group's case unquestioningly. For example, in Bloomfield the consultant architect used by CTA explained that:

> The residents' association wanted to keep everything in the area as it was. We said no, that everything progresses and there have to be some changes, otherwise the area would stagnate. We tried to introduce some changes which included some of the things they wanted in the community. But you can't keep a community in the same conditions all the time. Our aim was to keep the community together but drag it into the twentieth century. Anything that is done in Bloomfield has to be seen to last for 50–60 years.

The objectives were similar; the conflict was essentially about approach or method.

One project where objectives were not similar was CTA's sponsorship of a report by Alice Coleman on the Divis Flats complex in West Belfast. Local tenants had been campaigning for total demolition of the flats. CTA had read Coleman's (1985) book *Utopia on Trial* and invited her to carry out an evaluation of refurbishment versus redevelopment. She came down firmly in favour of the latter, supporting the tenants' struggle for demolition, which was recently successful.

Redevelopment, although comprising the first major projects CTA became involved in, was not typical of project work. Other project requests included design work for youth clubs, play centres, adventure playgrounds and community gardens. More recently the growing interest by community groups in local employment projects has led to increased requests for advice on the conversion of buildings to workshop units.

In processing project requests CTA works closely with the Community Architecture Committee of the Royal Society of Ulster Architects, which arranges for many projects to be undertaken which CTA could not assist with directly. Many requests concerning dampness were referred to a university physicist with a research interest in this area. CTA has been constantly seeking to develop such cooperation. Up to mid-September 1986, CTA had received 125 requests for assistance. 88 of these were 'problems' and 37 were 'projects'.

The initial discussions which accompanied the establishment of CTA envisaged that in addition to providing *reactive* practical help to community groups, the organization would take a *proactive* role about planning, housing and environmental issues. Limited staff resources and pressure to meet the range of practical problems thrown up by community groups held back the extent to which this work on issues and education occurred. However, a magazine was launched and CTA has been a focus for community education in planning, most notably in its recent work to involve community groups in issues raised by the preparation of a new development plan for the Belfast Urban Area.

The need for CTA

According to our survey, 85 per cent of community groups which used CTA during its first eighteen months approached the organization because they could not afford to use private consultants. 80 per cent of these user groups were satisfied or very satisfied with the assistance they received.

Of community groups that had not used CTA, 70 per cent stated that there was a need for such a service. For these groups, the most popular means of providing technical aid was stated as either through a voluntary organization (79 per cent) or through grants to community groups (78 per cent). When we put the same question to groups that had used CTA, 100 per cent supported provision through a voluntary organization and 62 per cent through grants to community groups. This indicates a high degree of satisfaction with provision through a voluntary organization.

Of the 318 environmental professionals (architects, planners, landscape architects and civil engineers) who responded to the survey, 84 per cent stated that there was a need for a technical aid service to community groups. The most popular means of providing such a service were through grants to community groups (75 per cent), through a voluntary organization (69 per cent) and through private consultants (62 per cent). Sixty-five per cent saw the area as a possible source of fee income.

The survey of Housing Executive District Managers found that of the 37 managers who replied, 92 per cent stated there was a need for technical aid, with 94 per cent supporting a voluntary organization as the most appropriate means. Of those managers who had had contact with CTA, 50 per cent described the service as good, 10 per cent as average, 20 per cent as variable and 10 per cent as bad. The survey of Divisional Planning and Development Officers found that of the five (out of seven) officers replying, four stated that technical aid for community groups was needed with most responses (three) favouring a voluntary organization. It is interesting that despite reservations about CTA's work, this population (state housing and planning officers) recorded the highest degree of support for community technical aid.

Summarizing a large amount of survey data, we found that there was a high level of agreement among community groups, environmental professionals, local politicians and housing and planning officers about the need for a community technical aid service in Northern Ireland and for CTA in particular. The most popular means of providing the service was a voluntary organization, although there was significant support among environmental professionals and community groups for a system of grants to enable groups to buy in assistance. We found a widespread view among community groups in both Protestant and Catholic areas that both opportunities and abilities to influence the actions of government bodies were lacking in Northern Ireland, that technical aid would improve this, and that more participation would benefit local communities and improve the efficiency and effectiveness of public bodies.

Conclusions

The extent of support for technical aid which we documented shows widespread agreement that it is a service that is needed in Northern Ireland. This support contrasts with the government's tentative attitude to the organization, probably because CTA is quite likely to perceive problems differently from senior levels of the state, where the main concern is often *control* in a deeply divided and unequal society.

Among the community groups, local politicians, housing managers and planners who expressed support for technical aid there are clearly different ideas about how such a service should operate. For example Housing Executive managers thought it should be an 'honest broker' rather than an advocate of the community group position.

CTA has been attempting to service a large number of requests for advice and assistance across Northern Ireland with 2–3 technical staff and several committed volunteers. It has managed to develop and deliver a range of services to a satisfactory standard from a small base, although a disproportionate amount of its work has been in Greater Belfast and on less demanding 'problems' rather than more demanding 'projects'. However CTA still lacks financial security and ability to plan ahead.

As part of the research we wanted to assess the broader significance of CTA. Through discussions we identified a number of recurring themes. A major one was how to get access to decision-making – a question of power, knowledge and resources. CTA could contribute to this by increasing the technical resources available to community groups, improving groups' organization of their work, improving their knowledge of 'the system', and facilitating alliances. Another major theme was that early participation in plans and projects would reduce the chances of conflict later on. However we found that community groups in both Protestant and Catholic areas (there are many more active ones in the latter) rarely saw the state as even a potential ally or enabler, except at one stage removed through grant-aid. State functionaries are neither educated nor expected to involve community groups in decisions.

CTA is essentially a democratic manifestation. This is considered in more detail by Blackman (1986). Its philosophy challenges present state structures in Northern Ireland. The state is not only a capitalist and, some would claim, a sectarian state, with all the implications that has for supporting projects based on progressive ideas about the distribution of knowledge, power and resources, but it is structured in a way that divides functions between different, sometimes competing, agencies. The holistic view of a community group about its area is not reflected in the structure of state agencies and so community action gets broken up and defused into official channels where it loses its holistic and collective nature. One result is that the causes of problems for the working class tend to be redefined on the state's terms: for example participation is accepted if it legitimates policy or shifts responsibility for social reproduction onto the working class's own resources (see Kraushaar, 1981). CTA, which suffers much less from these structural problems, has had to respond in a flexible and multidisciplinary fashion to problems encountered by community groups. We found such an adaptation to social reality a common feature of technical aid centres in Britain.

Ultimately what CTA seems to be about is people speaking and acting for themselves. But the extent to which the organization can support this depends, as always, on its sponsors. What is likely is that CTA will undertake a range of activities to attract funding, but some may be unpopular with some sponsors (see Lees and Mayo, 1984, for a discussion of these problems). The extent to which this undermines its progressive aspects depends on the backing it can maintain for such activities. This will probably involve CTA in arguments that some communities need to be equipped with technical resources so that their interests can be justly represented. This reflects an essentially pluralist conception of the state in Northern Ireland. However it is worth bearing in mind Weiner's conclusion about community action in Belfast in the 1970s:

> As a general rule, the more important an issue is to the needs of the ruling interests the less participation there is for those who might be opposed to it (Weiner, 1980: 152).

Note
This paper does not necessarily reflect the views of Community Technical Aid.

References

Association of Community Technical Aid Centres (1985) *Working with Local Communities*, London: ACTAC.

Blackman, T. (1986) 'The politics of place in Northern Ireland'. *International Journal of Urban and Regional Research* 10: 541–62.

Blackman, T. (ed.) (1987) *Community Based Planning and Development in Northern Ireland: Alternative approaches in architecture planning, health care and economic development*, Belfast: Policy Research Institute.

Blunkett, D. and Green, G. (1983) *Building from the Bottom: the Sheffield experience*, Fabian Tract 491, London: Fabian Society.

Boaden, N., Goldsmith, M., Hampton, W. and Stringer, P. (1982) *Public Participation in Local Services*, London: Longman.

Buchanan, G. (1986) 'Local Economic Development by Community Business'. *Local Economy* 2: 17–28.

Byrne, D. (1986) 'State sponsored control: managers, poverty professionals and the inner city working class'. In K. Hoggart and E. Kofman (eds) *Politics, Geography and Social Stratification*, London: Croom Helm.

Centre for Employment Initiatives (1984) *Beating Employment*, London: Centre for Employment Initiatives.

Coleman, A. (1985) *Utopia on Trial*, London: Hilary Shipman.

Collective Design/Projects (eds). (1985) *Very Nice Work If You Can Get It*, Nottingham: Spokesman.

Curtis, B and Edwards, D. (1980) *Planning Aid: An analysis based on the Planning Aid Service of the Town & Country Planning Association*, occasional Paper 1, Reading: School of Planning Studies.

Doyal, L. and Gough, I. (1984) 'A theory of human needs' *Critical Social Policy* 10: 6–38.

Evans, B. (1985) *Public Involvement in the Planning Process*, Research Paper 1, London: London Planning Aid Service.

Gardner, H.F., Crook, G. and Gomilny, J. (1982) *Public Involvement in the Planning Process: Walsall Area Planning Committees*, Birmingham: City of Birmingham Polytechnic Department of Planning and Landscape.

Goodwin, M. and Duncan, S. (1986) 'The local state and local economic policy'. *Capital & Class*. 27: 14–26.

Hester, R.T. (1984) *Planning Neighbourhood Space with People*, London: Van Nostrand.

Illich, I. et al. (1977) *Disabling Professions*, London: Boyars.

Kirkham, R. (1983) *Community Technical Aid Centre: Evaluation Report of the Pilot Project*, London: Town and Country Planning Association.

Kraushaar, B. (1981) 'Policy without protest: the dilemma of organising for change in Britain'. In M. Harloe (ed.) *New Perspectives in Urban Change and Conflict*, London Heinemann.

Lees, R. and Mayo, M. (1984) *Community Action for Change*, London: Routledge and Kegan Paul.

McArthur, A. (1986) 'An unconventional approach to economic development: the role for community business'. *Town Planning Review* 57: 87–100.

Morrison, C. (1986) 'CTA Progress Report'. *Catalyst* 11: 3–5.

Newham Docklands Forum (1983) *The Peoples Plan for the Royal Docks*, London: Newham Docklands Forum and GLC Popular Planning Unit.

Northern Ireland Assembly. (1983) *Report of the Environment Committee Inquiry into the Housing Executive Belfast Housing Renewal Strategy*, 2, volumes, Belfast: HMSO.

Northern Ireland Technical Aid Group. (1983) *Proposal for a Technical Aid Service in Northern Ireland*, Belfast: Northern Ireland Technical Aid Group.

Robertson, J. (1986). 'How the cities can finance new enterprise'. *Lloyds Bank Review* 161: 32–43.

Sewell, W.R.D. and Coppock, J.T. (1977). *Public Participation in Planning,* London: Wiley.

Skeffington Report (1969) *Report of the Committee on Public Participation in Planning: People and Planning*; London: HMSO.

Weiner, R. (1980) *The Rape and Plunder of the Shankill,* Belfast: Farset Co-operative Press.

Woolley, T. (ed.) (1985) *The Characteristics of Community Architecture and Community Technical Aid,* Occasional Paper 85/6, Glasgow: University of Strathclyde Department of Architecture and Building Science.

Woolley, T. (1987) 'Community Technical Aid: a new movement?'. In T. Blackman (ed.) *Community Based Planning and Development: Alternative approaches in architecture, planning, health care and economic development,* Belfast: Policy Research Institue.

11 'Doing the double' or doing without: the social and economic context of working 'on the side' in Belfast
Leo Howe

Although they were not designed to collect such information, many of the large-scale surveys of the unemployed (Hill et al., 1973; Daniel, 1974, 1981; White, 1984) have little or nothing to report on those working and claiming unemployment benefit. Many of the studies of the informal economy (Henry, 1978; Mars, 1982) in the 1970s also have little to say about the economic activity of the unemployed. Perhaps the best description available for the pre-1979 situation is that provided by Mardsen. According to him 'fiddling' generally starts when the unemployed have exhausted legitimate options and when financial and other pressures begin to escalate within the home. Working on the side takes the man out of the house, gives him something to do, and puts some money in his pocket. Such work is informally controlled by locals unwilling to see anyone do too well out of it. However even small amounts of earned income, together with benefits, were coming to be seen by some of Marsden's informants as a viable alternative to formal work (1982: 138–45, 198–200).

In recent work Pahl has argued that, for several reasons, the 'hidden' economy is in decline (1984: 93–8). One feature of this decline is the purported inactivity of the unemployed. Today, according to Pahl, the unemployed are too poor to work informally since they have not the money to buy tools nor can they afford to go to the pubs to make necessary contacts. In their Sheppey research Pahl and Wallace (1985: 208–9) found only one unemployed man (out of 26 in their total sample of 730 households) who was willing to admit to doing undeclared paid work. On the basis of their findings Wallace and Pahl (1986: 116) criticize Rose (1983) for arguing that high rates of unemployment create an incentive for unemployed individuals to invest more time in producing goods and services in the domestic economy, and Parker (1982) for asserting that high unemployment pushes people into the black economy. For Pahl the key to participation in all forms of work is employment status. Those in employment do more informal work both in the home and in the community than do the unemployed (1984).

While agreeing with much that Pahl argues, great care needs to be taken concerning the analysis of the paid work that the unemployed do. Other researchers have found more activity of this kind than has Pahl. Morris, for example, states that in Port Talbot, 'occasional work for undeclared income was relatively common' (1984b: 349, her emphasis) and was related to the size of individuals' social networks. Bostyn and Wight, working in Cauldmoss, Scotland, found that irregular work on the side was quite common and not described significantly differently from legitimate work (1984: 61-4; cf. Turner et al., 1985). The value of such work may be insignificant in relation to GDP but even small amounts of extra income can be important to individuals and, as Marsden implies, this may change a person's attitude to legitimate employment at times when jobs are scarce. It needs also to be mentioned that such practices may well vary from area to area according to local social and economic conditions: there is no reason to expect inner city areas in Liverpool or London to be similar to small towns; areas of very high unemployment to be the same as those of very low unemployment etc. Finally, there are, of course, severe methodological problems in obtaining reliable data on illegal activities and this needs to be taken into account when assessing particular findings.

Doing the double in Belfast
In Northern Ireland working for undeclared income while registered as unemployed or sick (and therefore claiming a state benefit) is colloquially known as 'doing the double'. The following is a basically descriptive account of the work that some unemployed do and the reasons why they do it. The data were gathered over a period of two years, by means of repeated interviews with, and observation of, forty working-class married men in two housing estates in Belfast, one Catholic (Mallon Park in west Belfast; unemployment rate at least 56 per cent) and one Protestant (Eastlough in east Belfast; unemployment rate at least 26 per cent).[1]

There are some interesting and significant differences between the unemployed in these two estates in terms of the extent of doing the double and the conceptualization of it. Thus, unemployed Catholics in Mallon Park do more undeclared paid work than their counterparts in Eastlough. Of the twenty unemployed in Mallon Park (most unemployed over two years) twelve have done a double at some time during their present spell of unemployment. For Eastlough where the informants have been jobless for just as long, the figure is eleven.[2] However the Catholics have, overall, worked for longer periods and earned more money than the Protestants. In addition Mallon Park residents tend to look for work in the black economy more actively and to evaluate such practices more positively that Eastlough residents. These differences are related to different historical and contemporary conditions in Catholic and Protestant areas of the city, and to various features of the sectarian divide. In brief these differences stem from: a more buoyant local economy in east Belfast where, because of the dominance of large firms and government administration, opportunities for doing the double are not great, and where residents are still oriented to legitimate jobs; a fragmented economy in west Belfast where manufacturing industry has collapsed and there are very few legitimate openings of any kind; heavy reliance on construction and services in west Belfast which sectors (particularly the former) are riddled with malpractice; a much more pervasive fear of informers (to the DHSS) in Eastlough than in Mallon Park; greater difficulty of surveillance by DHSS fraud investigators in west Belfast; opportunities for Catholics to work in the Republic of Ireland; and so forth. In short, whereas west Belfast provides very few opportunities for finding legitimate employment, there are better opportunities for doing the double. Conversely, residents of Eastlough are still oriented to the formal economy and hence do not appear to solicit for black economy jobs, and these anyway seem to offer fewer openings proportionately than in west Belfast. These contemporary conditions are related to the sectarian divide and the manner in which the larger Belfast economy has developed historically. In other words, the differences do not stem from the nature or characteristics of Catholics *qua* Catholics and Protestants *qua* Protestants, but are instead the outcome of the structures of opportunity and constraint in the two areas, which have in turn been produced by the manner in which sectarian ideology has shaped and been shaped by the industrial economy of Northern Ireland.[3]

Before proceeding it is necessary to point out that the paid work that is done by these unemployed only very rarely amounts to the money equivalent of a full-time job. Of the 23 cases doing (or having done) the double only one, a private taxi-driver, earns enough to enable him to sign off the register. All the other cases fall into one of four categories.[4] The first concerns those who have secured a short-term, one-off job. Danny Chapman obtained his one and only double nine months into his first spell of unemployment. One of his unemployed neighbours had been recruited to a squad of men to go down to the Republic to work on a building site. As more men were needed both Danny and another unemployed neighbour were asked to help out. They were all given transport to the south and each came back to Belfast the evening before his signing day (every fortnight), travelling back the next evening. Working six or seven days a week the job lasted three months and netted Danny a total of about £1500.

The second comprises those who obtain short-spell jobs at infrequent intervals. These are often in the construction industry. Neither Ray McGrath nor Eddie McCann have got anywhere near a legitimate job in the three years they have been unemployed, though both work irregularly on the side. Ray is a stand-by worker for a self-employed subcontractor who uses Ray, on the double, for about £75 (less than his weekly benefit) a week, whenever he is a man short. Ray has never worked in this way for more than three weeks at a time. Even if Ray wished to sign off, which he doesn't, his employer insists on him remaining on the register. Eddie McCann has had several small jobs tiling bathrooms and kitchens and once tiled a small supermarket. A final example is Dave Martin, a painter. Some eleven months after being made redundant a former employer asked if he wanted a few weeks work on the double at normal rates of pay. Whilst there, work continued to come in and the employer decided to keep Dave on in a legitimate capacity.

A third category comprises those who make work for themselves. Gerry Daly and a brother exploit a local dump for scrap metal; Martin Cavanagh sells wrapping-paper and cheap toys in the town centre in the weeks running up to Christmas: Jim Hughes distributed cards advertising his painting and decorating services and worked on and off for about a year; others babysit, mind children, act as catalogue agents (for the commission), collect beer cans and bottles, repair cars, dig gardens, etc.

The fourth category comprises those who obtain more permanent but part-time jobs. Brian O'Neil, scaffolder by trade, got a job driving a coal lorry on a part-time basis; some wives of unemployed men have undeclared part-time jobs as waitresses, shop assistants, cleaners, and so forth.

From the perspective of the unemployed several themes can be seen as structuring their ideas about doing the double. The first of these concerns the relation between benefits and wages. The point is this, and it is quite pervasive, unemployed men with dependent wives and children will rarely admit their willingness to take a job that does not provide them with an income significantly greater than their benefits. The crucial aspect of their argument is that a wage must cover more than benefits:

> Why should I work for £5 or £10 a week [i.e. over and above the dole].
> It might get me out of the house, but there's no point me coming in on
> a Friday and putting £60, £70 on the table. She'll scream at me just the
> same as she does now. I might be in a job and it might be better than
> sitting here but if it's not paying me what's the bloody point?

And:

> She was complaining about the bad wages, you know, me handing her
> £50 on a Friday night, but now if you're arguing the wife would say to
> youse, 'I wish you'd go out and get a job', . . . but sure you're still in the
> same boat. She's complaining about very little money now. It was still
> the same when I was working.

Those stating a willingness to work in low-paid jobs tend to be
Protestants (marginally), older (thus no dependent children), have a
wife in work, or who are extremely depressed and bored (in which
case it is the activity of work more than the lack of money which is
the motivating force to take low-paid jobs), or some combination of
these.

A corollary of the contention that wages must cover more than
benefits is the theme that wages for a job should stand on their
own, that is, there should be no need to claim low income benefits.
It is often argued that wages requiring such benefits cannot be fair
wages and that therefore the jobs must be dead-end jobs with no
promotion prospects, little opportunity for overtime, probably short-
term, etc. Most therefore assert they might just as well be on the
dole as in such employment. Taking such jobs is tantamount to
moving from the unemployment trap to the poverty trap. In short,
they see very little financial difference between being unemployed
and supported by one set of benefits, and being in a low-paid job
which necessitates a different set of benefits to underpin the wages,
(See Dennehy and Sullivan, 1977; and Turner et al., 1985 for
similar information from Liverpool and Cauldmoss respectively).

One of the major items a wage should cover is the earner's
'pocket-money'. Few employed men hand over the whole of their
wage-packets to their wives. The most common form of allocation
for working men is to supply the wife with 'her wages' (a sum of
money for the upkeep of the house) retaining the rest for a variety
of purposes. While there is wide variation in who pays for what the
common core is that the husband divides the cake keeps some for
his own personal use. The ideology behind this is that those who
receive a wage *earn* it, that is, *deserve* it; they have *worked* for it, it
is the exchange for what they do in their place of employment. Part
of this money is earmarked for the financing of the household, and
part is kept to be disposed of in any way the earner sees fit. What is
important to the man is what this enables him to do. In Northern

Irish working-class culture this often means liberal use of pubs, clubs, pool rooms, betting shops, etc.

It is this premium over the dole that is so sorely missed in unemployment and low-paid jobs, for it is precisely in these cases (cf. Morris, 1984a: 501) where household income is passed in toto to female control. Those going from low-paid jobs to unemployment experience little change in income allocation as both wages and benefits are held by the wife. Those moving from higher-paying jobs, in which the male has controlled the money, to unemployment experience either an abrupt change or very difficult marital relations, or both if really unfortunate. Those attempting to retain control over the benefit, giving the wife only a proportion and keeping some back for personal spending money face frequent altercations and outside condemnation. Figures suggest that the great majority of unemployed men (26 out of the 31 who do not have working wives) have very little control over their benefit: many simply sign the Giro for the wife to cash. What this evidence clearly indicates is a normative view that the principal claim on income is the financing of essential household and communal expenditure. Whatever the source of the income an element is earmarked for this and, given the pattern of gender roles in Belfast, is controlled by the wife.

In unemployment, benefit income is handed over to female control not only because it is too small for any to be retained, but also because it is not conceived of as having been earned through work, and this means the claimant husband has no normatively supported right to use part as personal spending money. This is why many unemployed assert that the benefit is nothing to do with them, or that it is not theirs, or that it does not belong to them.

Given these facts it becomes clear why many unemployed men insist that a job must carry wages which are greater than benefit. It can be readily seen, furthermore, that any income derived from doing a double will alleviate many of the difficulties precipitated by the change from work to unemployment. The income, first of all, is earned by work, usually outside the house, and therefore in a location conceptually equivalent to a place of employment; it is in short a partial return to the sphere of employment. The move back into the world of work, however far removed from the 'real' thing, redefines the person not only as someone who can work, who has skills, who has contacts and friends, but also as someone willing to work, someone not content to sit on his backside doing nothing. It therefore re-establishes him in a viable status with a role that provides a valuable identity (Kelvin, 1980: 301; Kelvin and Jarrett, 1985: 42–8).

The move into 'employment' is simultaneously a move out of the domestic sphere where in large measure the unemployed man is an unwanted intruder who disrupts household routines; for most 'housewives' the loss of work[5] for their husbands leads to an unacceptable invasion of their daytime space and privacy. The mere physical separation of the spouses can serve to enhance their relationship, but a separation based on the man working the double actually reproduces the sought after complementarity and interdependence associated with a legitimate job.

In general, doing the double provides, even if in attenuated fashion, some of the latent functions of work described by Jahoda (1979). If the double is done for an employer the worker has a time-structure imposed on him, and even if he works for himself he still must work to a schedule which requires planning and organization. Working, of course, enforces activity and this is undoubtedly one its main benefits. So many of the unemployed have little to do and complain of the aching boredom, the numbing inactivity and the impotence of just sitting. The double may not entail regularly shared experiences and contacts with people outside the home, but if often does, and this supplies the worker with a new and changing fund of stories with which to regale family and friends. In order to buttress a work indentity slowly slipping away as the time from the last job inexorably increases, the man doing the double no longer has to fall back on stale, oft-repeated anecdotes gained from that job, but can now tell jokes and relive events that happened very recently.

Doing the double then provides various intrinsic rewards: it reduces boredom and depression; increases activity; allows working skills to be exercised; widens horizons; creates and maintains contacts outside the home; re-establishes working status; and enhances a self-image. Additionally, of course, it also brings in much-needed income.

In order to assess the significance of any income earned it is necessary to place it in the context of replacement ratios. I define the replacement ratio as the ratio of total net income from all sources when head-of-household is unemployed to total net income from all sources when head-of-household is in work. For several reasons which cannot be discussed here, the computation of such ratios is very difficult. Let me just put on record here that the average replacement ratio for the twenty unemployed from Mallon park is 86 per cent, and for the twenty unemployed from Eastlough it is 78 per cent, which two figures reasonably reflect the fact that Protestants in east Belfast tend to be in higher skilled and better paying jobs. What is striking, however, is just how high the figures are: seven of the Mallon Park unemployed have present incomes within £15 of their previous in-work incomes, and five of these have been unemployed less than one year. It is low pay then which characterizes these figures, not generous benefits. Male manual workers in Northern Ireland have consistently had to work longer hours for less money than their counterparts in Great Britain (Black et al., 1980: 7), and even if wages and salaries in Northern Ireland have recently grown relative to those in Britain, net disposable income per capita is still substantially lower: in 1978 it stood at 81 per cent of the UK average (Gibson and Simpson, 1981). There is little doubt therefore that the unemployed would take legitimate jobs provided that they could get wages that would give them this £15 to £20 premium over the dole, but especially in west Belfast such jobs no longer exist. Those that are available are often temporary or part-time or job schemes for the unemployed or very low paid. The married man with dependent children will find himself no better off at all, and possibly even worse off, should he take such a job. It is easy to see therefore why the unemployed look for jobs on the double. The situation is somewhat different in Eastlough: because of the relative lack of opportunities, the fear of informers, and the greater commitment to the formal economy which, it is hoped, will eventually produce good jobs again, the unemployed look less hard than the Catholics or, at least, encounter fewer opportunities.

In default of satisfactory wages from reasonable jobs many Catholics in Mallon Park will do a double whenever they can, and the income they obtain gives them that premium they require. Thus Gerry Daly averages about £35 a week recycling scrap. For two months his wife did a double on a local delivery round earning £20 a week at best. Frank Connolly, the taxi-driver, can earn up to £100 a week. Even if Ray McGrath only does three or four, three-week stints in one year this has the effect of raising his income by around £15 a week; and this is probably the value of the doubles that many of the others (Eddie McCann, Martin Cavanagh, for example) do. The doubles that the Protestants of Eastlough have done increase weekly income less than this for they work less frequently.

Apart from registered unemployed earning realistic wages on the double (while there was only one of these in my sample in Mallon Park I knew of several others in the estate who were in virtual full-time doubles), none of this work would be worth it if the income was to be declared to the DHSS, as only £4 of such income is disregarded in calculating benefit entitlement. What would be the point of Martin Cavanagh standing in the cold selling wrapping paper for up to ten hours a day if, in earning £70 in a (good) week he loses £66 of his benefit? He only does it in the first place so as to be able to have a relatively decent Christmas, to buy toys for his children and to take his wife out. And much the same can be said for others who do the double to this extent. (Incidentally, the Supplementary Benefit Commission argued that benefit levels should be high enough to allow people to lead a comparatively normal existence [cf. Howe 1984].) Such work does not in any sense provide remuneration which can remotely substitute for social security benefits (Cavanagh only earns £70 a week for three or four weeks in the year), and therefore the work is not a viable alternative to the dole. In most cases the jobs are feasible because those doing the work have the safety cushion of their benefits. The income obtained from such work is therefore perceived as a supplement to benefit income and not as a rival to it. Put another way, benefit income, viewed as wholly inadequate (Clark, 1978; Evason, 1980), is not conceived of as a substitute for wages, but as something which itself has to be supplemented (Howe in press).

Those doing the double also argue that they are not scrounging since they put so much effort into the work that they do. Gerry Daly has to work six or seven days a week just to make £30 to £40; it is because their time is a cheap resource that they are willing to spend large amounts for small returns. They do not see themselves as parasites from another point of view as well. The unemployed, particularly of Mallon Park, whether doing the double or not, have come to consider jobs on the side as a viable way of financing households, largely because they have simultaneously become accustomed to seeing their local economy in a permanently depressed condition and their local labour market offering only the very poorest paid jobs. Were the economy to begin providing jobs of the kind they once had there is little doubt that they would return to them, giving up the doubles in the process. In other words those doing the double may be commended as good entrepreneurs: despite appalling constraints on their lives they are willing to do almost any type of work to earn enough money to make life on the dole more tolerable.

As mentioned earlier, Pahl has argued that in the 1980s, 'unemployed people are too poor to work informally: they cannot go to the pubs to make essential contacts, and they cannot afford the tools and equipment to do such odd jobs as decorating or car repairs' (1984: 96). The evidence from Belfast is such as to place doubt on this rather sweeping generalization. None of the doubles thus far described was the result of a pub contact. In many cases doubles (like those of Cavanagh and Daly) are based on individual enterprise. Where intermediaries have been important such people are often kin or friends and neighbours living in the same area. None of this means that doubles are never acquired by contacts in the pubs, but the notion that the pub is the best place for making such contacts cannot be sustained. The point surely is that job information and allocation flow along already existing networks, and so long as these are maintained and serviced they may well pay dividends. Those who have failed to get doubles tend to have few contacts and relatives in the estate and indeed come from small families (Morris, 1984b; Bostyn and Wight, 1984). That they have few marketable skills outside factory employment is a further disadvantage. Those who have obtained jobs either have large families with many relatives in local areas, or have a wide circle of friends and acquaintances, or have specially useful skills, or a combination of some of these.

Of course, people can ply their trade only if they have the requisite tools and equipment. But many tradesmen will have acquired such minimum tools as are necessary whilst they were at work. Plumbers, electricians, joiners, plasterers, mechanics, tilers, etc. usually build up a stock of tools over the years, and the jobs they may obtain when unemployed assist them in maintaining this stock. Moreover there are many jobs requiring no tools. An unemployed person does not need any resources, save time, to be a child-minder, a bar doorman, a scrapdealer, a night security guard, a cleaner, a shop assistant, and many others.

Just because an area may be suffering chronic high unemployment this is no reason to think that local demand for services will be completely depressed. In fact, it is precisely because many people have so little money that they will use the services of the unemployed before those of legitimate firms, since the former will be cheaper. And the money that the unemployed earn helps in maintaining demand: the money that Gerry Daly earns enables him to hire the services of a neighbour, on the double, to build a new brick fireplace; the money that Joe Carlin earns helping to build extensions along the Falls Road enables him to buy carpets for his house and to use an unemployed tiler to fit them for him. It is not the case that the poor are, in general, too poor to work informally. Those doing the double, especially in Mallon Park, repeatedly remark that it is their abject poverty which provides them with the incentive to search for and solicit informal work. What makes the difference between one area and another are the prevailing structures of opportunity and constraint, and these are not, it would seem from the Belfast case, related only to the performance of the economy. What also needs to be taken into account are various social and cultural processes (Howe, in press), and on this score Pahl's analysis of Sheppey is rather weak.

There can be little doubt anymore that the unemployed living on supplementary benefit have a very difficult time trying to make ends meet. Many are in debt; many have to borrow from relatives who may well themselves be subsisting on one or another state benefit; many suffer from their transactions with the supplementary benefit system in which attempts to claim benefits they feel entitled to can be fraught with problems (Howe, 1985); many find that their weekly benefit lasts for six or even five days only; many never go out, never buy new clothes, can only afford inadequate fuel supplies and exist on poor food; many find themselves living a life of grinding poverty in which adults have to sacrifice themselves to protect their children from the depredations of such a penny-pinching existence. Given the almost total lack of viable jobs in Belfast it is no wonder that unemployed married men and women will seek to augment their income in any way that they can. The relatively small amounts that are earned individually are unlikely to add up to more than a small fraction of the total of goods and services comprising the 'informal' economy, the major part of which is probably accounted for, as Pahl rightly argues, by those already in legitimate jobs. But to the unemployed individuals concerned such amounts can make all the difference between living and mere subsistence.

And of course, it is not only the unemployed who benefit from these practices. Many employers prefer to use labour on the double because they reap numerous advantages: they pay no National Insurance contributions, no sick pay, no holiday pay, no redundancy money, no compensation for industrial injuries, they often pay lower wages as these are not subject to the usual deductions, they can lay off workers at a moment's notice and know they can hire them quickly, and they can ignore the trades unions. Because of this many employers will only take on workers if they are prepared to remain as officially unemployed. This is particularly the case in the construction sector (especially house-building) where subcontractors use a great deal of labour on the double (Howe, in press). Many of the jobs described in this chapter could not have been worked other than on the double; unemployed people trying to get jobs, especially short-term ones, are expected by their prospective employers to remain on the unemployment register and to continue to draw benefit, and if they are not prepared to do this there are others who are. Since there are so few legitimate jobs, since the income is always welcome and since a double job may be one route back into the formal economy, few unemployed are willing to pass up opportunities which may only occur at infrequent intervals. One might speculate moreover that the state is itself not too bothered about the situation: the fines for employers colluding in this practice are no higher than for the unfortunate 'employees' who have no alternative but to comply with a system they help to reproduce but from which they gain so little.

For many of the unemployed then, and especially those in Mallon Park and west Belfast generally, doing the double is seen as probably the only way to circumvent a deeply entrenched and debilitating system of industrial wage labour. Hedged in on all sides by a virtual total lack of legitimate and viable jobs (again more so in west Belfast), exploiting employers, low wages, iniquitous taxes, inadequate benefits and high prices for fuel, food, transport and clothing (Jefferson and Simpson, 1980) the unemployed in a depressed economy perceive that they have very little option: they either do the double or do without.

Notes

1. 'Mallon Park' and 'Eastlough' are pseudonyms, as are all the names of individuals used in the text.
2. Which is, or course, not to say that over 50 per cent of the unemployed are doing the double at any one time. Accurate rates are impossible to compute since the situation changes rapidly and many doubles last only a short time.
3. Because of the very sensitive nature of the issues involved, and because lack of space permits only a cursory analysis, interested readers are strongly advised to consult Howe (1984; 1985; in press; n.d.). For a more complete analysis of the difference between Catholics and Protestants as regards doing the double, see Howe (in press). For some similar data obtained by other researchers in Northern Ireland, see Jenkins (1978) and Morrissey et al. (1984); see also Jenkins and Harding (1986) for a review of the literature on informal economic activity in the province. It perhaps should be added that Jenkins argues that doing the double was more prevalent in his area of research, Ballyhightown, than it appears to be in Eastlough (Jenkins and Harding, 1986: 30-1), and that Irish colleagues of mine, basing their views on anecdotal evidence, also claim that doing the double is more prevalent in east Belfast than my own data would seem to suggest.
4. These categories are merely descriptive and have no analytical value. In practice, jobs on the side form a continuum from the one-off, short-term job to the full-time, five-day-a-week job, the vast majority though falling in the former part of this continuum. Additionally what people count as a double (and there are many other terms to describe these practices) varies quite a lot.
5. Work is here defined narrowly and from the largely male perspective as 'employment'. Such definitions do, of course, lead to domestic conflict (McKee and Bell, 1986: 142-3).

176   *Northern Ireland: studies in social and economic life*

References

Black, B., J. Ditch, M. Morrissey and R. Steele (1980) *Low Pay in Northern Ireland*, London: Low Pay Unit.
Bostyn, A. and D. Wight (1984) 'From cole to dole: ethnography of an ex-mining village in central Scotland'. *Proceedings of the Association for Scottish Ethnography* 1, 47–69.
Clark, M. (1978) 'The unemployed on supplementary benefit'. *Journal of Social Policy* 7, 385–410.
Daniel, W.W. (1974) *A National Survey of the Unemployed*. London: PEP (Political and Economic Planning).
Daniel, W.W. (1981) *The Unemployed Flow: stage 1 interim report*, London: Policy Studies Institute.
Dennehy, C. and J. Sullivan (1977) 'Poverty and unemployment in Liverpool'. In F. Field (ed.), *The Conscript Army*, London: Routledge & Kegan Paul.
Evason, E. (1980) *Ends That Won't Meet*, London: Child Poverty Action Group.
Gibson, N.J. and J.E. Spencer (1981) 'Unemployment and wages in Northern Ireland'. In B. Crick (ed.) *Unemployment*, London: Methuen.
Henry, S. (1978) *The Hidden Economy: the context and control of borderline crime*, London: Martin Robertson.
Hill, M., R. M. Harrison, A. V. Sargeant and V. Talbot (1973) *Men Out of Work*, Cambridge: Cambridge University Press.
Howe, L. E. A. (1984) 'The unemployed on supplementary benefit'. *Scope* 76, 12–14.
Howe, L. E. A. (1985) 'The 'deserving' and the 'undeserving': practice in an urban, local social security office'. *Journal of Social Policy* 14, 49–72.
Howe, L. E. A. (in press) 'Unemployment, doing the double and local labour markets in Belfast'. In C. Curtin and T. Wilson (eds) *Ireland From Below: Social change and local communities in modern Ireland*, Galway: Galway University Press.
Howe, L. E. A. (n.d.) *Jobs, Wages and Benefits: an anthropological study of unemployment in a divided society* (in preparation).
Jahoda, M. (1979) 'The impact of unemployment in the 1930s and the 1970s'. *Bull. Brit. Psychol. Soc.* 32, 309–314.
Jefferson, C. W. and J. V. Simpson (1980) *The Cost of Living in Northern Ireland*, Belfast: Northern Ireland Consumer Council.
Jenkins, R. (1978) 'Doing the double'. *New Society*, 20 April.
Jenkins, R. and P. Harding (1986) *Informal Economic Activity in Northern Ireland: a review of the literature*, University College of Swansea, Dept of Sociology and Anthropology.
Kelvin, P. (1980) 'Social psychology 2001: The social psychological bases and implications of structural unemployment'. In R. Gilmour and S. Duck (eds) *The Development of Social Psychology*, London: Academic Press.
Kelvin, P. and J. Jarrett (1985) *Unemployment: its social psychological effects*, Cambridge: Cambridge University Press.
Mars, G. (1982) *Cheats at Work: an anthropology of workplace crime*, London: George Allen & Unwin.
Marsden, D. (1982) *Workless*, London: Croom Helm.
McKee, L. and C. Bell (1986) 'His unemployment, her problem: the domestic and marital consequencies of male unemployment'. In S. Allen, A. Waton, K. Purcell and S. Wood (eds) *The Experience of Unemployment*, London: Macmillan.
Morris, L. (1984a) 'Redundancy and patterns of household finance'. *Sociological Review* 32, 492–523.
Morris, L. (1984b) 'Patterns of social activity and post-redundancy labour-market experience'. *Sociology* 18, 337–52.
Morrissey, M., T. O'Connor and B. Tipping (1984) 'Doing the double in Northern Ireland'. *Social Studies* 8, 41–54.
Pahl, R. E. (1984) *Divisions of Labour*, Oxford: Basil Blackwell.

Pahl, R. E. and C. Wallace (1985) 'Household work strategies in economic recession'. In N. Redclift and E. Mingione (eds) *Beyond Employment: household, gender and subsistence,* Oxford: Basil Blackwell.

Parker, H. (1982) *The Moral Hazards of Social Benefits,* London: Institute of Economic Affairs.

Rose, R. (1983) *Getting by in the Three Economies,* University of Strathclyde, Centre for the Study of Public Policy.

Turner, R., A. Bostyn and D. Wight (1985) 'The work ethic in a Scottish town with declining employment'. In B. Roberts, R. Finnegan and D. Gaillie (eds) *New Approaches to Economic Life,* Manchester: Manchester University Press.

Wallace, C. and R. Pahl (1986) 'Polarisation, unemployment and all forms of work'. In S. Allen, A Watson, K. Purcell and S. Wood (eds) *The Experience of Unemployment,* London: Macmillan.

White, M. (1984) *Unemployment and Labour Markets* London: Policy Studies Institute.

12 Youth culture and the youth service in Northern Ireland
Wendy Garner, Norman Gillespie and Tom Lovett

Youth and community in west Belfast

Since 1969 Northern Ireland has witnessed widespread social, economic and political upheaval on a scale previously unprecedented. Part of this process is a result of the transformation in the economic structure of the province and part due to the related political crisis (the 'Troubles'). West Belfast in particular has been subject to massive changes in the physical, economic, social and political spheres. In the physical sphere it has witnessed the largest redevelopment programme in the history of Northern Ireland and the creation of an infrastructure geared towards the 'new' market relations ('urban motorways', 'supermarkets', 'enterprise zones'). The local economies have been virtually destroyed (the Shankill itself lost 9000 jobs between 1968 and 1980) in the interests of British, European and American economies of scale. Social life has been transformed by the mass dispersal of families, a loosening of informal neighbourhood ties, increasing secularization, and the influx of mass, ready-made entertainments ('slot machines', 'leisure centres', 'video', 'pool rooms') and the decline of participatory entertainments (with the emphasis on people rather than machines).

Politically, the area has witnessed the dismantling of the 'Orange System' with the fragmentation of the Unionist Party and the rise of Sinn Fein. It has also witnessed the shift towards militant political stances and the growth of paramilitary organizations and activities. The area also experienced some of the worst street confrontations between Catholics and Protestants, sectarian murder campaigns, the Provisional Irish Republic Army's 'armed struggle' against the 'British presence' and the sharp end of the 'British presence' itself – British Army patrols on the streets, 'blanket searches' 'internment', 'plastic bullets', 'Diplock courts' and 'supergrasses'. West Belfast is now almost totally segregated into a Catholic part (the Greater Falls) and a Protestant part (the Greater Shankill). Understandably the attitudes of the people in the communities have changed correspondingly, e.g. attitudes to family and neighbourhood, to the opposite sex, to religion and morality, to work (or lack of it), to social life, to the army and the police, to the 'other sort'. Nowhere is the conflict and tension, the paradoxes and the contradictions, resulting from this upheaval, more apparent than in the lives of working-class youth.

It was no coincidence therefore that the period 1968–80 saw the mushrooming of 'community' work in all its many manifestations and the extension of formal youth provision. The state was heavily involved in both developments. The 1970s did, in fact, see a tremendous growth in community activity and new, dynamic and progressive forms of voluntary effort in Northern Ireland. As one prominent 'community worker' put it:

> Pressure for social change came from a range of different sources inspired by a variety of motives, including compassion for victims of misfortune, anger at injustice, and fear of unrest. Thus, literally hundreds of local self-help community and pressure groups have emerged over the past decade – some to protest at local conditions (e.g. Save the Shankill) and some to try and meet immediate needs (e.g. lunch clubs, summer schemes, play groups). At the other end of the scale government, motivated by a mixture of fear at social unrest and concern for the worst extremes of poverty and deprivation, backed community programmes (e.g. increased expenditure on community work, Belfast Areas of Need, etc.). In the middle lots of concerned and compassionate individuals became involved in organizations such as those running children's holiday schemes, helping the elderly and so on. (Frazer, 1981b: 14)

The watershed of community development and action in the province had arrived by the end of the decade. It was reached with the growth of 'Community Workshops' (YOPs, YTPs) for the training of unemployed young people. The Department of Manpower Services and later the Department of Economic Development encouraged the growth of such projects. Resources and the responsibility for managing these were given to community groups in the professed hope that training would be more relevant than that available in the Government Training Centres.

What in effect such projects constituted was a fairly cheap means of social control (however 'well-meaning' the organizers of such schemes). It was a peripheral strategy designed to encourage young people to accept their powerlessness rather than confront it. Management committees faced with the dilemma of pursuing 'radical alternatives' or adopting conservative means of organization, content, etc. have found themselves opting for the latter to ensure their own continuance, As one commentator has stated:

This has meant the perpetuation of the belief that the development of entrepreneurial capitalist skills is an essential element in bringing about a vital economic life within the province. Pradoxically, those who would wish to radically change society are being used to maintain the most cherished and outmoded beliefs of the status quo. Out of the most sincere motivation and because of the need to actually be doing something about the ills of this society many find themselves bound and tied. (Deane, 1981: 17).

Many of those involved in these developments in youth and community work hoped that they might be a means of improving relations between Catholic and Protestant communities by stressing the common social and economic issues faced by both communities. However, there was a contradiction in using community development as a means of improving community relations. Neighbourhood community associations and projects tend to be parochial in nature. The function of such groups is to win as many scarce resources as possible for their community. This inevitably means that people in other neighbourhoods get less. When neighbourhoods are sectarian ghettos to begin with, this means that, willingly or not, the competition for resources (which may be based on parochial considerations) inevitably has sectarian implications.

The same is also true of local youth provision and there has been a growing concern with the state of youth in west Belfast since 1969 when young people increasingly came to the fore in the street confrontations and paramilitary violence which has permeated Belfast for the last 17 years. Prior to 1969 specific youth initiatives were rare in the province. In the Shankill, for instance, they were confined mainly to 'uniformed' organizations, a few church groups and the odd Girls' Club Union or Boys' Club. The activities were mainly drill, physical activities and games, religious observance and, in the case of the 'uniformed' groups, 'badge work'. Formal youth work in Ballymurphy was non-existent prior to 1970 and its eventual development was the result of a community organization initiative closely followed by a rival church group. Direct state youth provision in the two areas is relatively new.

The form of youth developments has often centred on 'giving young people something to do' – assuming that by occupying the recipients with 'acceptable alternative forms of behaviour' the aspiration to riot or engage in other 'anti-social' behaviour such as mugging, solvent abuse or drinking will somehow magically disappear. There have been many other approaches, most notably attempts at 'integrated holidays', 'inter-club visits', and the general development of a 'non-sectarian' ethos in youth provision.

The state and working-class youth culture

Attempts at somehow controlling working-class youth by the state are, of course, nothing new and have exhibited various degrees of success from the inception of the 'quasi-military' youth brigades of the turn of the century to the purpose built leisure centres of today. Such efforts have tended to be concerned mainly with giving working-class youth 'something constructive to do' (see Hall and Jefferson 1976: 176). The more recent sophisticated attempts at curbing the informal activities of youth are a reflection of the changing social and economic climates. Urban redevelopment and the destruction of local economies have clearly left their mark. On the one hand, there is the reality of the erosion of the traditional working-class neighbourhood and community itself and all that went with it. On the other hand, there was the failure to deliver the promised 'consumer society' which the increased geographical and educational mobility – not to mention changes in production – were to bring. Working-class youth activities became and remain the most pressing 'moral panics' (See Cohen, 1973) of the age of mass youth unemployment in 'ghost towns' which were originally designed as 'growth towns'. The changes in the shape of 'informal' youth activities are a direct reflection of the breakdown of the close interconnection between family and neighbourhood and the weakening of informal society controls (see Hall et al. 1978: 156-7). There has been a strong tendency to reduce this complex and uneven process to the famous, and simplistic, 'generation gap'.

Part of this process has been the re-orientation of the working class away from a general concern with their own well-being and basic needs to a more specific consumerism which can best be summed up by reference to the increased working-class demand for material goods. Working-class youth have similarly been subject to this process. 'We have become dependent on capitalism,' as one commentator has put it (Seabrook, 1983: 193). In his classic study of the working class, Hoggart drew attention to the responsibility of the minority of political activists and convinced trade unionists within the working class:

> I have recalled their work for social reform and have stressed that it was inspired not primarily by a search for material goods but by a sense of the need for higher satisfactions by working people, satisfactions which could be more easily obtained once material improvements have been made ... [their] ideas ... are in danger of being lost ... material improvements can be used so as to include the body of working people to accept a mean form of materialism as a social philosophy. (Hoggart 1976: 322-3).

This is exactly what has happened to the working-class due to the relative increase in prosperity since the war. Material satisfactions have become the end rather than the means to achieving higher aims such as: access to a higher quality of life generally, culture, peace, a healthy environment, satisfactory relationships, higher standard of education, real power and participation in the political system, safe and comfortable working conditions, and meaningful work. The drive to achieve such standards in life has been largely lost to the vast majority of the working class because of the changes in social priorities over the past thirty years. One is reminded of the passage in *The Ragged Trousered Philanthropists* when the cynical charge hand of the house decorators tells the trade unionist, Owen, 'Them things aren't for the likes of us' (Tressel, 1985). It is such an attitude which comes dangerously close to stagnating the growth of working-class consciousness and undoubtedly plays a large part in the seemingly hopeless drive for escapism which has come to dominate working-class culture in the 1980s. Formal youth work probably reaffirms this position.

Working-class youth culture is often represented in terms of a distinctive 'sub-culture' (often implying a 'delinquent' sub-culture). However, it should be stressed that the dominant elements of that youth culture are often the same elements that dominate working-class culture in general (the 'parent' culture) albeit in varying degrees of manifestation. Anyone who decided, for instance, to describe a gang of 'mods' or 'punks' in the Shankill or Ballymurphy would be seriously misleading if they attempted to present this as an indication of the dominant youth culture in those areas. Such recognizable 'sub-cultural' groups tend to be peripheral, sparse and grossly unrepresentative of working-class youth culture in general. The unattached youth on the Shankill, i.e. the 70 per cent *not* attending some form of youth provision, frequently referred to 'mods' and 'punks' as 'queers', 'dick heads', 'eejits', and so on. Clarke et al. (1976) have drawn attention to the fact that: 'We must ... see sub-cultures in terms of their relation to the wider class culture networks of which they form a distinctive part. When we examine this relationship between sub-culture and the "culture" of which it is a part we call the latter the "parent" culture ...' (p. 13). This should not be confused with the particular relationship between 'youth' and their 'parents'. What it means is that a sub-culture, though differing in important ways – in its 'focal concerns', its 'trends' and its activities – from the culture from which it derives, will also share some things in common with that 'parent' culture. The overwhelming desire for money, obsession with 'the other sort' (blacks, taigs, prods, etc.) are forms of escapism which are often associated with the working class in general. Youth sub-cultures must first be related to the parent cultures of which they are a sub-set. But sub-cultures must also be analysed in terms of their relation to the dominant culture – the overall disposition of cultural power in the society as a whole. We may distinguish 'respectable', 'rough', 'delinquent' and the 'criminal' sub-cultures within working-class culture but, although they may differ amongst themselves, they all derive in the first instance from a 'working-class parent culture'. They are all, therefore, subordinate sub-cultures in relation to the dominant middle class or bourgeois culture.

It should be stressed that the great majority of working-class youth never enter a tight or coherent sub-culture at all. Individuals may, in their personal life-careers, move into and out of one, or indeed several, sub-cultures. Their relation to the existing sub-cultures may be fleeting or permanent, marginal or central. The sub-cultures are important because in them the response of youth takes a peculiarly recognizable form. But in the post-way history of the class, these may be less significant than what young people do most of the time. The relation between the 'everyday life' and the 'sub-cultural life' of different sections of youth is an important question in its own right.

Working-class youth culture in west Belfast

It would be absurd to attempt an analysis of working-class youth culture in west Belfast without placing it firmly within the social and economic and political transformations briefly outlined at the beginning of this chapter. The impact of redevelopment on the local economy (particularly in the Shankill) has many similarities with Cohen's analysis of east London sub-culture and his exploration of the 'intra-class dynamic between youth and parents' (Cohen 1972). As in east London, redevelopment and rehousing led to a depopulation of the area, and the break-up of the traditional neighbourhood. There was a massive drift in the workforce from areas like Shankill to the new so-called 'growth centres' outside Belfast. The most immediate impact was on the kinship structure – the fragmentation of the extended family and its partial replacement by the more nucleated 'families of marriage'. Cohen has described how the new housing projects in East London had the effect of destroying: 'the function of the street, the local pub, the corner shop, as articulations of communal space. Instead there was only the privatised space of the family unit . . . in total isolation . . . which lacked many of the informal social control generated by the neighbourhood . . .' (Cohen 1972: 16). Alongside this was the drastic reconstruction of the local economy – the decay of small craft industries, their replacement by the larger concerns often situated outside the area, the decline of the family business and the corner shop. This has many similarities with studies of the Shankill (Wiener 1980: Gillespie 1983).

Cohen saw the formation and development of youth sub-cultures as latent attempts to express and resolve the contradictions which such forces left in the parent culture. He suggested that such sub-cultures represented an 'imaginary relation' (ideologically speaking) between the social reality of working-class youth and the 'real relations' (objective structural reality). Cohen's position allows for an analysis in which specific economic and political forces (de-industrialization, redevelopment, powerlessness) create the conditions in which sub-cultures can emerge. Furthermore, this position allows for an analysis whereby working-class sub-cultures possess a 'relative autonomy' of their own. This means that although they may have specific conditions of existence, it does not necessarily follow that their actions are given directly by those conditions. It is the sub-culture relation to the wider class formation which is the crucial determinant. This overcomes the problem of ideology which is so often ignored in non-sociological accounts of sub-cultures and youth in general.

This position places one in a situation to analyse the informal structure of ideological practices which are not directly given by the economy. In the Northern Ireland situation there is a specific combination of national, racist, labour aristocratic and ethnic ideologies (not given by the economy) which determine the particular form of ideological social relations. This is what prevented the assimilation of Protestants into the Irish nation and sustained 'pro-British' Protestant ideology. This in turn sustained minority antipathy and produced militant republicanism. Here we have *specific* economic and political conditions (plantation, uneven development of capitalism, partition) creating the conditions in which (but not necessitating) two forms of nationalism, a cross-class political alliance, i.e. Unionism, and a labour force divided on ethnic identification, emerged.

It is quite common for unemployed youths from the Shankill to describe their plight in terms of 'all the Taigs coming up from the South and getting all the good jobs'. This, of course, has no foundation in *objective reality* but it is undoubtedly grounded in the *social reality* of the subject and its consequences will undoubtedly be *real*. Thus working-class youth sub-cultures in west Belfast reflect the divisions in their respective 'parent' communities.

Hall et al. have indicated how those working-class sub-cultures take shape at the level of the social and cultural class-relations of the subordinate classes. They have agreed that they are one of a number of strategies (negotiation, resistance, struggle) adopted by the working class to counter its subordinate position and that a developed and organized revolutionary working-class consciousness is only one among many such responses and that it must be seen as such (Hall et. al., 1978: 440-5). To define everything else, i.e. Protestant working-class Unionism, as a token of incorporation, imposed an abstract scheme on to a concrete historical reality.

We must attempt to show how, under what conditions, the class has been able to use its material and cultural 'raw materials' to construct a whole range of responses. Some such responses – the repertoire of resistance specific to the history of the working class – form an immense reservoir of knowledge and power in the struggle of the class to survive and win space. Working-class sub-cultures serve to 'win space' for the young: cultural space in the neighbourhood and institutions, real time for leisure and recreation, actual room on the street or the street corner. They serve to mark out and appropriate 'territory' in the localities. They form around key occasions of social interaction – the weekend, the discos, the bank holiday trip, the 'night out' the 'standing about doing nothing' of the weekday evening, the Saturday match, the eleventh (of July night), the anniversary of internment. They cluster around particular locations. They develop specific rhythms of interchange, structured relations between members, younger to older, experienced to novice, stylish to square. They explore 'focal concerns' central to the inner life of the group; things always 'done' or 'never done', a set of social rituals which underpin their collective identity and define them as a 'group' instead of a mere collection of individuals.

While different sub-cultures provide for a section of working-class youth (mainly boys) one stragegy for negotiating their collective existence they cannot resolve the problems of subordinate class experience. This can be 'lived through', negotiated or resisted but it cannot be *resolved* at that level. There is no 'solution in the sub-culture' for problems fused by the key structuring experiences of the class. There is no 'sub-cultural solutions' to working-class youth unemployment, educational disadvantage, compulsory miseducation, dead-end jobs, the routinization and specialization of labour, low pay and the loss of skills.

Working-class sub-cultures are a response to a problematic which they share with other members of the 'parent' class culture. But class structures the adolescent's experience of that problematic in distinctive ways. First, it locates the young at a formative stage of their development, in particular material and cultural milieux, in distinctive relations and experiences. These provide the essential cultural frameworks through which that problematic is made sense of by the youth. This 'socialization' of youth into a class identity and position operates particularly through two 'informal' agencies: family and neighbourhood.

Family and neighbourhood are the specific structures which form, as well as frame, youths' early passage into a class. For example, the sex-typing roles and responsibilities characteristic of a class are reproduced, not only through language and talk in the family, but through daily interaction and example. In the Northern Ireland context the home is where primary socialization into sectarianism is located:

> The Catholics have big families and they won't work. Daddy says we are poor because the Government takes his money to give to the Catholics and all their children and their priests to keep them in luxury because they don't work. In the South they wouldn't get any money and would have to work for it. Here they keep us all poor and don't appreciate what they get. (Fraser, 1973: 96).

In the neighbourhood, patterns of community solidarity are embedded partly through the structure of interactions between older and younger youth/children. It is largely through friends and relations that the distant but increasingly imminent worlds of work or of face-to-face authority (the rent man, social security, the police and army) are appropriated. Through these formative networks, relations, distances, interactions, orientations to the wider world and its social types, are delineated and reproduced in the young.

Working-class youth like their parents, inhabit a distinctive structural and cultural milieu defined by territory, objects and things, relations, institutional and social practices. In terms of kinship, friendship networks, the informal culture of the neighbourhood, and the practices articulated around them, the young are already located in and by the 'parent' culture. They also encounter the dominant culture, not in its distant, remote, powerful, abstract forms, but in the located form and institutions which mediate the dominant culture to the subordinate culture, and thus permeate it. Here, for youth, the schools, work, leisure are the key institutions and agencies of public social control. The school serves this function, but alongside it, a range of institutions, from the 'hard' coercive ones, like the police, to the 'softer' variants – youth and social workers.

Youth culture as a whole must be understood, then, as a response to the problems posed by a framework of bourgeois institutions but that response in west Belfast is the response from a divided working-class experience of those institutions. The problem is to decide in what sense that response equals resistance and under what circumstances that resistance has political implications.

In west Belfast there is undoubtedly a specific working-class youth response which equals resistance and has political implications. Amongst certain sections of Protestant youth it is a resistance to the perceived threat posed to Protestant survival by militant republicanism. In catholic west Belfast it is an 'armed revolutionary struggle' against the perceived injustices of British imperialism. Thus resistance in west Belfast is not the 'resistance through ritual' of sub-cultural youth groups in Great Britain. Any political analysis of youth culture in west Belfast must focus on the culture's 'divided working classness' rather than on its youthfulness (Corrigan and Frith, 1978: 236-7).

This is not to deny that young people are in a 'special' situation (largely because of their relative – and only relative – freedom from family and occupational ties) but *emphasizing* this makes political analysis impossible. For a start it means exaggerating the differences between youth culture and its class context at the expense of the continuities. The concept of 'generation gap' (derived from theories of middle-class youth) is inappropriate and incorrect for working-class teenagers. Even if they are involved with *different institutions* from their parents (schools, youth clubs), the evidence is that their response to them is based on similar values. A focus on the youthfulness of youth culture means a focus on the psychological characteristics of young people – their adolesence, budding sexuality, individual uncertainties and so on – at the expense of their sociological characteristics, their situation in the structure of the social relations of capitalism.

Working-class young people are, in sociological terms, an actual and potential labour force and it is this (not their youth) which determines their social situation and structures their institutional relationships. And it is this which unifies their diverse experiences and links them to their elders and gives their culture its political potential.

All relevant institutions must also be connected in any sociological annalysis of youth culture just as they are in working-class experience. The reality of the teenage world is the combination of family and school, apprenticeship and job, police and courts, youth clubs and social workers and commerce and mass media, and it is this combination to which youth culture is a response. We should stop trying to isolate youth culture with respect only to commercial leisure or to the school or the law. It is no accident that the institutional components of youth culture match the Althusserian list of state apparatuses (Althusser 1971).

Youth provision in west Belfast

Given the analysis offered above we need to consider how youth provision in west Belfast relates to the cultural needs and aspirations of working-class youth in a society riven by poverty, unemployment, sectarian divisions and violent conflict. The aims of the youth service in the province are wide and varied –

> to develop a working partnership between young people and older adults through the youth group in the context of the family and wider community, to provide opportunities for the greater participation by young people in the planning and management of their own activities as a means of finding their place in the community, to give young people an opportunity to express their views to promote a greater understanding of a society with diverse traditions and approaches and a willingness to communicate positively within it. (Youth Committee for Northern Ireland 1981: 7)

Such statements resound with the familiar themes of liberal consensus approaches to youth and community work, i.e. partnership, participation, opportunity, understanding, communication, 'finding their place in the community'. There is no reference here to youth *questioning* their place in the community. The latter is rarely if ever perceived in terms of working-class community. Rather it is the community of all the interests in society.

One needs to consider how such statements square up with the reality of working-class life and youth work provision in Northern Ireland and particularly in west Belfast. Our research into youth provision in that part of the city offered an opportunity to answer the question by looking at the reasons why only one third of the youth population made use of the youth service. The research took place with the active support and advice of community groups in these two communities and involved a combination of qualitative and quantitative research methods, i.e. questionnaires and related ethnographic studies with a range of young people, participants and non-participants in the youth service.

This examination of participants and non-participants in formal and informal youth provision in west Belfast presented us with much more than an explanation of why some young people were attracted to organized youth groups and some were not. The picture presented reflected also the tensions and implications of a complex web of social relations which had a particular form and content representing the underlying social structure of west Belfast. This culture of working-class youth in Ballymurphy and Shankill encapsulates the social, economic and political characters of the two communities which may be seen in terms of a peculiar ethic identification.

If we first of all consider the position of non-participants (at least two-thirds of the total) it is at once apparent that the 'youth service' fails to meet their needs. In fact it does not claim to provide for them. As one senior administrator in the service admitted: 'We recognize that not all that is provided by youth clubs or organisation is acceptable to all young people.' For the participants, the service claims to offer 'personal development', 'social education', 'recreation' and 'reconciliation'. However, our investigations have revealed that most young people who do attend clubs, do so first and foremost for games and physical activities. Our investigations have further revealed that youth clubs are basically in the business of social control (the participants were clearly aware of this) – 'getting the kids off the streets'. 'Personal development', 'social education', and so on are the 'official' terms for the different methods of achieving what is in effect 'character-building' (conformity).

When we proceed to consider the position of the 'non-participants' it becomes apparent that they are not 'uncontrollable', 'unattached', 'undersirables', 'anti-social', or 'hoods'. Their culture is an expression of their social locality and includes divergent forms of social activities as well as complex sets of attitudes and ideas which articulate divergent experiences in relation to national aspirations, oppression and political affiliations against a background of widespread social and economic upheaval and deprivation. The culture of working-class youth in west Belfast therefore includes a variety of 'negative' manifestations of behaviour associated with the failure of society to provide or allow for many of the basic desirable objectives in life.

It is important, however, not to generalize about their culture. As we have indicated above, too many studies have tended to focus on a particular group or a few groups of young people in a given community and these are taken as being representative of youth in general. In the Shankill and Ballymurphy we encountered multiple forms of 'culture' representing many different groups and individuals. There were widely divergent attitudes and social status between the groups but also within them.

We also must consider what is perhaps the largest group of young people of all. That is, those who don't belong to the 'corner gang', 'drinking club' 'flute band', football team', etc. but who spend most of their spare time in informal activities at home (watching television, playing records) or participating in the local adult culture. This consists of mirroring the social activities of one or other parent (going fishing with 'Da', visiting relations) and/or participating in the parental role.

We must be clear, however, and stress that, despite an affinity to the local adult culture in west Befast in ethnic and political terms, the relationship between youth and adults has been severely undermined by the tensions arising out of changes in the structure of working-class communities. Urban redevelopment and the destruction of local economies have clearly left their mark. This has, among other things, led to an erosion of the more informal agents of social control.

This process has largely been the product of attempts to promote a greater emphasis on individual freedom. This concept, however, involved a negative veiw of freedom which represented a move towards an atomistic structure of society which would include an embourgeoisement of the working class. This, of course, backfired as the major aspect of the restructuring of the British and Irish economies since the war has been large industrial wastelands with previously unparalleled unemployment rates. The embourgeoisement thesis remained the pipedream it always was.

The most glaring characteristic of the culture (apart from a preoccupation with the political crisis) is the overriding desire for 'money' which is clearly associated with 'success'. The aims of life are not viewed in terms of those things which contribute to a higher quality of life. They represent what can best be described as 'vulgar consumerism' which is a product of a 'consumer society' which has failed to 'deliver the goods'. Success is translated into goals which are realistically obtainable depending on the position of the individual locally and economically. This may include 'successfully' mugging an old woman. This interpretation of success (which is a product of society) cannot be accommodated by formal youth clubs (which are supposed to cater for the *needs* of young people in society).

The tensions inherent in the youth/adult relationship exhibit themselves perhaps most clearly when one examines the local adult reaction to each cycle of 'moral panic' in the community. It is the 'concerned' and 'upstanding' elderly citizens who are usually first to advocate 'conscription', 'flogging', 'kneecapping' and a host of even more hideous punishments which at times defy the imagination. Paramilitary organizations in both communities in West Belfast have practised such policies in response to such panics regularly.

All too often local reactions, 'official' commentators and the media have concentrated on narrow negative conceptions of youth culture (i.e. vandalism, joyriding, theft, rioting) without considering its many positive features. The complexities of the problem are often lost in the search for 'simplistic' explanations and solutions to the problems of urban working-class society. In our work with young people we discovered a sensitive and at times an unselfish humanism even in those young people who would be considered 'problematic' 'deviants', 'hoods' or worse. Even the 'rakers' in our study were concerned with events in the Third World, the 'bomb', and 'the Troubles'.

Conclusions

The existing youth service has little or no relevance to the culture and the issues and problems facing a large section of young people in that part of the city. Little will be achieved by more of the same. The service is still in many respects deeply rooted in a traditional view of working-class youth and a response which places a high priority on old-fashioned discipline, controlling and regulating behaviour.

With a few exceptions it takes little notice of the tremendous changes which have taken place in the life of working-class youth and the communities they live in. It does little to meet the real needs of the latter and, given its structure and philosophy, it may be that it never will. However, there is an opportunity to make real meaning out of terms like 'youth and community work'. This would require a more open commitment to the local community to act as an important educational resource and service for youth and adults alike. They could, in cooperation with the local community, provide a youth and community service which centred on the real problems facing such communities. Reports in the past have stressed the need for community-based education centres. Such centres could seek to break the artificial division between youth and adults; to offer an education which helps them to reflect on their community and its influence on their attitudes and values; to provide the skills necessary for community regeneration and restructuring. Our research into youth culture in Northern Ireland has stressed that community relations will not be improved by inter-community visits or dialogue. It must start with a process which helps both communities to examine themselves, *their* culture, *their* history, *their* attitudes. The youth service in Northern Ireland, if it was prepared to grasp the nettle, could play an important role in this process.

References

Althusser, L. (1971) 'Ideology and the state'. In *Lenin, Philosophy and Other Essays*, London: New Left Books.

Clarke, T., Hall, S., Jefferson, T. and Roberts, B. (1976) 'Subcultures, cultures and class'. In Hall and Jefferson (1976).

Cohen, P. (1972) 'Subcultural conflict and working-class community', *Working Papers in Cultural Studies* 2, Birmingham, Centre for Contemporary Cultural Studies.

Cohen, P. (1973) *Folk Devils and Moral Panics*, London: Paladin.

Corrigan, P. and Frith, S. (1976) 'The politics of youth culture'. In Hall and Jefferson (1976).

Deane, E. (1981) 'Community work in the seventies'. In Frazer (1981a).

Fraser, M (1973) *Children in Conflict*, Harmondsworth: Pelican.

Frazer, H. (ed.) (1981a) *Community Work in a Divided Society*, Belfast: Farset.

Frazer, H. (1981b) 'Speech given at International Voluntary Service Workshop, Glencree'. In Frazer (1981a).

Gillespie, N. (1983) *Shankill Employment Report*, Belfast: Shankhill Community Council.

Hall, S., Critcher, C. Jefferson, T., Clarke, J. and Roberts, B. (1978) *Policing the Crisis*, London: Macmillan.

Hall, S. and Jefferson, T. (eds) (1976) *Resistance through Rituals*, London: Hutchinson.

Hoggart, R. (1976) *The Uses of Literacy*, Harmondsworth: Pelican.

Seabrook, J. (1983) *Unemployment*, London: Granada.

Tressel, R. (1985) *The Ragged-Trousered Philanthropist*: London, Panther.

Wiener, R. (1980) *The Rape and Plunder of the Shankill*, Belfast: Farset.

Youth Committee for Northern Ireland *(1981) Report for Period 1977–1981*, Belfast: HMSO.

Index

agricultural industry
 beef, 41–4
 cereals, 53
 dairying, 37–41
 employment in, 35, 76
 pigs, 46–51
 poultry and eggs, 50–52
 sheep, 44–6
Althusser, L., 187
Anglo-Irish Agreement, 113
Association of Community
 Technical Aid Centres,
 150–51

Ballygowan (Co. Down), 28
Ballyhightown, 175n3
Ballymoney (Co. Antrim), 28
Bannock, G., 104
Barritt, D.P., 5
beef industry, 41–4
Belfast, 19
 and CTA, 155
 'doing the double' in, 165–75
 manufacturing firms in, 105–24:
  demand structure, 115–
  24; distribution of supply
  and demand, 108–14;
  supply structure, 105–8
 Queen's University, 11, 27
 youth and community in,
  178–80, 183–91
Bell, C., 175n5
Black, B., 82, 171
Black, J.B.H., 127, 137
Blackman, T., 153, 161
Blunkett, D., 150
Boaden, N., 149
Bolton Report, 103
Bostyn, A., 165, 173
Braid Valley (Co. Antrim), 28
Bryson, G.H., 27
Buchanan, G., 150
Buchanan, R., 18
Bull, P.J., 87, 88, 89, 94

Burton, F., 7, 9
Business Week, 105
Butlin, 56
Byrne, D., 150
Byron, R., 56, 63

Cabinet List, 92–3
Carter, C.F., 5
Cawley, M., 30
Census Atlas, 31
Centre for Employment Initiatives,
 150
Centre for the Study of Conflict,
 20, 22
cereal growing, 53
Clark, D., 98
Clark, M., 172
Clarke, T., 182
Cohen, P., 181, 183–4
Collective Design/Projects, 150
Common Agricultural Policy
 (CAP), 35–7
communal divide
 development of, 3–4
 and 'doing the double', 165–6
 and NI economy, 12–13
 sectarianism, 13, 14, 16, 178,
  186
 and social research, 5–12, 13–16
Community Technical Aid (CTA),
 149–61
 conclusions on, 160–61
 context of, 153–5
 development of, 155–9
 need for, 159–60
 origins of, 150–52
Compton, P., 31
Confederation of British Industry
 (CBI), 78, 103
Continuous Household Survey,
 7, 31
Coppock, J.T., 149
Cormack, R.J., 14
Corrigan, P., 187

193

Printed and bound in Great Britain at
The Camelot Press Ltd, Southampton